BRAZILIAN RECIPES

TASTE BRAZIL AT HOME WITH AUTHENTIC AND EASY BRAZILIAN RECIPES

By
BookSumo Press
Copyright © by Saxonberg Associates
All rights reserved

Published by
BookSumo Press, a DBA of Saxonberg Associates
http://www.booksumo.com/

ABOUT THE AUTHOR.

BookSumo Press is a publisher of unique, easy, and healthy cookbooks.

Our cookbooks span all topics and all subjects. If you want a deep dive into the possibilities of cooking with any type of ingredient. Then BookSumo Press is your go to place for robust yet simple and delicious cookbooks and recipes. Whether you are looking for great tasting pressure cooker recipes or authentic ethic and cultural food. BookSumo Press has a delicious and easy cookbook for you.

With simple ingredients, and even simpler step-by-step instructions BookSumo cookbooks get everyone in the kitchen chefing delicious meals.

BookSumo is an independent publisher of books operating in the beautiful Garden State (NJ) and our team of chefs and kitchen experts are here to teach, eat, and be merry!

INTRODUCTION

Welcome to *The Effortless Chef Series*! Thank you for taking the time to purchase this cookbook.

Come take a journey into the delights of easy cooking. The point of this cookbook and all BookSumo Press cookbooks is to exemplify the effortless nature of cooking simply.

In this book we focus on Brazilian food. You will find that even though the recipes are simple, the taste of the dishes are quite amazing.

So will you take an adventure in simple cooking? If the answer is yes please consult the table of contents to find the dishes you are most interested in.

Once you are ready, jump right in and start cooking.

— BookSumo Press

TABLE OF CONTENTS

About the Author. 2

Introduction 3

Table of Contents 4

Any Issues? Contact Us 10

Legal Notes 11

Common Abbreviations 12

Chapter 1: Easy Brazilian Recipes 13

    Brazilian Street Plantain 13

    Homemade Piri Piri 15

    How to Make Dulce de Leche 17

    Manioc Parmesan Bites 19

    (Pao de Queijo) 19

    Porto Alegre Salsa 21

    Rabanada 23

    (Alternative French Toast) 23

    Brazilian Fruit Shots 26

    Collard Green Skillet 28

    South American Avocado Smoothie 30

    Brigadeiro 32

(Mini Chocolate Truffles) 32

Maria's Parmesan Chili Croquettes 34

Chicken Taquitos and Homemade Guacamole 36

Bolo de Biscoito de Limão 39

(Lime Biscuit Cake) 39

Spicy Coconut Glazed Chicken 41

Brasileiro Rice 44

Easy Homemade Churrasco 46

Brazilian Long Grain 48

Bolo de Banana 50

Brazilian Lunch Special 52

(Black Beans with Chicken) 52

3-Ingredient Sun Salad 54

Cod and Coconut Stew 56

Sao Paulo Poundcake 58

Sweet and Salty Raisin Rice 60

Classic Dry Beef Chuck and Coconut Stew 63

South American Seafood Soup 66

Rice Skillet with Orange and Pimento 69

Brazilian Vegetarian Hot Pot) 71

(Ginger and Coconut Curry 71

Black Bean Stew I 74

Steak with Chimichurri	76
Fortaleza Stroganoff	79
Eveline's Latin Lasagna	81
Coconut Shrimp Pot	84
Mushrooms Brasileiro	87
Bananas Assadas Quentes	89
Tropical Mango Stew	91
Ensalada de Papas I	93
How to Roast Brazilian Nuts	95
Onion Salad South American	97
Chipotle Beans Stew with Rice	99
Salvador Chicken Stew	102
Brazilian Sausage	105
Spicy Pink Shrimp	107
Potato Salad Brazilian II	109
Brasileiro Skirts	111
Ambrosia Pudding	113
Habanero Rice	115
Feijoada II	117
(Full Black Bean Stew)	117
Brasileiro Flank	120
Lime Glazed Sirloin	122

Goya Recaito and Seafood Stew 125
Caramelized Bananas 127
Spanish Rice Fritters 129
Mushroom Strogonoff South American 131
Bananas do Amor 133
Latin Tip Roast 135
Camarão de Coco 137
Carrot Cake with Cocoa Glaze 139
How to Grill a Steak Brazilian Street Style 142
Caribbean Tilapia Stew 145
Rice Apple Shrimp Salad 148
Brazilian Long Grain II 150
Garlicky Chicken with Mango Salsa 152
Brazilian Shrimp Skillet 155
Latin Flavored Butter 157
Catalina's Comfort Cake 159
Summer Night Banana Coffee Smoothie 162
Savory Pineapple Steaks 164
Brazilian Wild Rice 166
Latin Leeks with Sweet Vinaigrette 168
Vegetable Fiesta 170
Caribbean Jumbo Stew 173

Simple Portuguese Torte 175

South American Street Cocktail 177

Brazilian Pot Pies 179

Homemade Barbeque Sauce 182

Vanilla Pie 184

Flan 101 186

Chicken Cutlets with Chili Sauce 188

Banana Cloves 191

Brazilian Casserole 193

(Shrimp, corn, and Parmesan and Peppers) 193

Brazilian Potatoes 196

Thursday's Latin Lunch Box Salad 198

Kielbasa Stew 200

Creamy Coconut Cassava and Shrimp 203

Chipotle Shrimps 205

Pumpkin Bonbons 207

Brazilian Strawberry Tart 209

Spicy Salmon Fillets 211

Simple Brazilian Long Grain III 213

Estofado de Pescado 215

(Coconut Sea Stew) 215

Zesty Veggies and Potato Salad 218

THANKS FOR READING! JOIN THE CLUB AND KEEP ON COOKING WITH 6 MORE COOKBOOKS.... 220

Come On... 222

Let's Be Friends :) 222

ANY ISSUES? CONTACT US

If you find that something important to you is missing from this book please contact us at info@booksumo.com.

We will take your concerns into consideration when the 2nd edition of this book is published. And we will keep you updated!

— BookSumo Press

Legal Notes

ALL RIGHTS RESERVED. NO PART OF THIS BOOK MAY BE REPRODUCED OR TRANSMITTED IN ANY FORM OR BY ANY MEANS. PHOTOCOPYING, POSTING ONLINE, AND / OR DIGITAL COPYING IS STRICTLY PROHIBITED UNLESS WRITTEN PERMISSION IS GRANTED BY THE BOOK'S PUBLISHING COMPANY. LIMITED USE OF THE BOOK'S TEXT IS PERMITTED FOR USE IN REVIEWS WRITTEN FOR THE PUBLIC.

COMMON ABBREVIATIONS

C.(s)	C.
tbsp	tbsp
tsp	tsp
oz.	oz.
pound	lb

*All units used are standard American measurements

Chapter 1: Easy Brazilian Recipes

Brazilian Street Plantain

Ingredients

- 4 very ripe plantains (black skin)
- cooking spray

Directions

- Before you do anything, preheat the oven to 450 F.
- Grease a baking sheet with a cooking spray. Discard the plantain peel and slice it into 1/2 diagonal pieces.
- Lay the plantain pieces on the baking sheet. Cook it for 14 to 16 while flipping it halfway through.
- Once the time is up, allow the plantains slices to cool down completely then serve them.
- Enjoy.

Servings Per Recipe: 4

Timing Information:

| Preparation | 5 mins |
| Total Time | 20 mins |

Nutritional Information:

Calories	218.3
Fat	0.6g
Cholesterol	0.0mg
Sodium	7.1mg
Carbohydrates	57.0g
Protein	2.3g

* Percent Daily Values are based on a 2,000 calorie diet.

Homemade Piri Piri

Ingredients

- 4 tbsps lemon juice
- 5 tbsps olive oil
- 1/4 C. vinegar
- 1 tbsp cayenne pepper
- 1 tbsp garlic, minced
- 1 tbsp paprika
- 1 tsp salt
- 1 tbsp chili flakes

Directions

- Get a medium mixing bowl. Combine in it all the ingredients.
- Use this sauce to coat you chicken with it before grilling or roasting it in the oven. Serve it warm.
- Enjoy.

Servings Per Recipe: 1

Timing Information:

| Preparation | 5 mins |
| Total Time | 1 hr 20 mins |

Nutritional Information:

Calories	692.0
Fat	70.6g
Cholesterol	0.0mg
Sodium	2468.4mg
Carbohydrates	17.6g
Protein	3.4g

* Percent Daily Values are based on a 2,000 calorie diet.

How to Make Dulce de Leche

Ingredients

- 1 can sweetened condensed milk

Directions

- Use a sharp knife of a bottle opener to pierce the top of the milk can.
- Remove the paper from the can and discard it.
- Place a large saucepan over medium heat. Place in it the milk can and pour it in the saucepan enough water to cover 1 inch of the can.
- Wrap a small piece of oil on top of the can and let it cook for 4 h over low medium heat.
- Once the time is up, discard the foil and open the milk can. Serve your dulce de leche with some cut up fruits, crackers...
- Enjoy.

Servings Per Recipe: 1

Timing Information:

| Preparation | 2 mins |
| Total Time | 4 hrs 2 mins |

Nutritional Information:

Calories	171.6
Fat	4.6g
Cholesterol	18.1mg
Sodium	67.9mg
Carbohydrates	29.0g
Protein	4.2g

* Percent Daily Values are based on a 2,000 calorie diet.

Manioc Parmesan Bites
(Pao de Queijo)

Ingredients

- 2 C. sweet manioc starch
- 1 C. milk
- 1/2 C. margarine
- 1 tsp salt
- 1 1/2 C. grated parmesan cheese
- 2 eggs

Directions

- Before you do anything, preheat the oven to 400 F.
- Place a medium saucepan over medium heat. Stir in it the milk, salt, and margarine. Cook them until they start boiling.
- Turn off the heat. Stir in the starch into the milk mix until no lumps are found.
- Combine the eggs with cheese into the mix then mix them well with your hands until you get a soft dough.
- Shape the dough into 1 to 2 inches balls and place them on a lined up baking sheet.
- Cook the cheese bites in the oven for 8 to 14 min or until they become golden brown. Serve them hot with your favorite dip.
- Enjoy.

Servings Per Recipe: 1

Timing Information:

| Preparation | 20 mins |
| Total Time | 40 mins |

Nutritional Information:

Calories	87.8
Fat	7.6g
Cholesterol	26.9mg
Sodium	297.2mg
Carbohydrates	0.9g
Protein	3.9g

* Percent Daily Values are based on a 2,000 calorie diet.

Porto Alegre Salsa

Ingredients

- 1 large onion, diced
- 1 large tomatoes, peeled, seeded and diced
- 2 tbsps red wine vinegar
- 2 garlic cloves, minced
- 1 -2 tbsp olive oil
- 1 tsp dried parsley
- 3 drops chili sauce
- salt, as needed
- pepper, as needed

Directions

- Get a large mixing bowl: Combine in it all the ingredients and stir them to coat.
- Place the sauce in the fridge for sit for at least 1 h. Serve it right away.
- Enjoy.

Servings Per Recipe: 2

Timing Information:

| Preparation | 10 mins |
| Total Time | 10 mins |

Nutritional Information:

Calories	112.4
Fat	7.0g
Cholesterol	0.0mg
Sodium	8.1mg
Carbohydrates	12.2g
Protein	1.7g

* Percent Daily Values are based on a 2,000 calorie diet.

Rabanada

(Alternative French Toast)

Ingredients

- 1 medium sweet baguette
- 3 large eggs
- 3/4 C. sweetened condensed milk
- 6 tbsps whole milk
- 1/2 tsp vanilla extract
- 1/2 tsp kosher salt
- 1/2 C. granulated sugar
- 1 tbsp unsweetened cocoa powder
- 1/4 tsp ground cinnamon
- 3 -4 C. vegetable oil

Directions

- Slice the bread into 1 inch slices.
- Get a large mixing bowl: Mix in it the eggs, condensed milk, whole milk, vanilla extract, and salt. Whisk them well.
- Dip the bread slices completely in the eggs mix and cover the bowl with a piece of plastic wrap.
- Place a large pan over medium heat and heat 4 C. of vegetable oil in it.
- Drain the toast slices and cook them in the hot oil for 2 to 4 min on each side or until they become golden brown.

- Get a shallow dish: granulated sugar, cocoa powder and cinnamon. Coat the toast slices with the sugar mix then serve them warm.
- Enjoy.

Servings Per Recipe: 4

Timing Information:

Preparation	7 hrs
Total Time	7 hrs 15 mins

Nutritional Information:

Calories	1844.8
Fat	173.2g
Cholesterol	161.2mg
Sodium	436.4mg
Carbohydrates	67.5g
Protein	12.1g

* Percent Daily Values are based on a 2,000 calorie diet.

Brazilian Fruit Shots

Ingredients

- 2 tsps granulated sugar
- 1 lime
- 2 1/2 oz. cachaças
- 8 berries
- 1 -2 tbsp mango
- 1 -2 tbsp pineapple

Directions

- Place the lime wedges in a small mixing bowl. Sprinkle the sugar over the limes wedges and crush them with the back of a spoon.
- Spoon the mix to a cocktail shaker and to it the cachaça. Shake them well then pour the mix in a glassed filled with ice cubes.
- Serve your cocktail with your favorite toppings.
- Enjoy.

Servings Per Recipe: 1

Timing Information:

| Preparation | 10 mins |
| Total Time | 10 mins |

Nutritional Information:

Calories	213.1
Fat	0.1g
Cholesterol	0.0mg
Sodium	2.1mg
Carbohydrates	15.4g
Protein	0.4g

* Percent Daily Values are based on a 2,000 calorie diet.

Collard Green Skillet

Ingredients

- 2 lbs collard greens
- 2 tbsps olive oil
- 1 tbsp butter
- 1/3 C. minced shallot
- 1 tbsp minced garlic
- kosher salt and pepper

Directions

- Remove the stems of the collard greens and slice them into thin strips.
- Place a large skillet over medium heat. Melt the butter in it. Sauté in it the garlic with shallot for 2 min.
- Stir in the collard greens and cook them for 12 to 14 min or until they are done. Adjust the seasoning of your stir fry then serve it warm.
- Enjoy.

Servings Per Recipe: 8

Timing Information:

Preparation	5 mins
Total Time	25 mins

Nutritional Information:

Calories	78.4
Fat	5.2g
Cholesterol	3.8mg
Sodium	31.8mg
Carbohydrates	7.0g
Protein	2.6g

* Percent Daily Values are based on a 2,000 calorie diet.

South American Avocado Smoothie

Ingredients

- 1/2 avocado
- 1 1/2 C. milk
- 1/2 C. ice
- 3 tbsps sugar

Directions

- Get a food processor: Combine in it all the ingredients and blend them smooth.
- Serve your smoothie right away.
- Enjoy.

Servings Per Recipe: 1

Timing Information:

Preparation	5 mins
Total Time	6 mins

Nutritional Information:

Calories	541.3
Fat	28.1g
Cholesterol	51.2mg
Sodium	190.3mg
Carbohydrates	63.3g
Protein	14.0g

* Percent Daily Values are based on a 2,000 calorie diet.

BRIGADEIRO

(MINI CHOCOLATE TRUFFLES)

Ingredients

- 1 (14 oz.) cans sweetened condensed milk
- 1 tbsp butter
- 3 tbsps cocoa
- chocolate sprinkles

Directions

- Place a heavy saucepan over medium heat. Combine in it the condensed milk with cocoa powder and butter. Mix them well.
- Let them cook for 16 to 20 min until the mix becomes thick.
- Coat your palms with some butter and scoop some of the mix in your hands then shape it into a 1 1/2 inches balls. Place it on a lined up baking sheet.
- Repeat the process with the remaining mix to make more balls. Place them in the fridge to rest for at least 10 then serve them.
- Enjoy.

Servings Per Recipe: 40

Timing Information:

| Preparation | 5 mins |
| Total Time | 20 mins |

Nutritional Information:

Calories	35.9
Fat	1.1g
Cholesterol	4.1mg
Sodium	15.1mg
Carbohydrates	5.6g
Protein	0.8g

* Percent Daily Values are based on a 2,000 calorie diet.

Maria's Parmesan Chili Croquettes

Ingredients

- 2 oz. butter, cubed
- 2/3 C. flour
- 1 egg, separated
- 1/4 C. breadcrumbs
- 1/4 C. parmesan cheese
- salt and pepper, as needed
- 1 tbsp water
- salsa for serving

Directions

- Before you do anything, preheat the oven to 350 F.
- Get a large mixing bowl: Combine in it the butter with flour and mix them well with your hands until it becomes coarse.
- Combine the egg yolk, breadcrumbs, parmesan cheese, salt and pepper, and water into the flour mix until you get a smooth dough.
- Shape the mix into bite size pieces balls and coat them with the egg white. Place them on a greased cookie sheet.
- Cook the beach bites in the oven for 26 min. Flip the balls and cook them for an extra 5 min. Serve them warm with your favorite dip.
- Enjoy.

Servings Per Recipe: 4

Timing Information:

| Preparation | 15 mins |
| Total Time | 45 mins |

Nutritional Information:

Calories	249.4
Fat	15.0g
Cholesterol	88.8mg
Sodium	244.6mg
Carbohydrates	21.1g
Protein	7.1g

* Percent Daily Values are based on a 2,000 calorie diet.

Chicken Taquitos and Homemade Guacamole

Ingredients

- 3 C. shredded cooked chicken
- 2 tsps lemon juice
- 1 tsp cumin
- 1 jalapeno, diced
- 2 tbsps chopped cilantro
- 2 garlic cloves, minced
- 1/2 C. Monterey jack cheese, shredded
- salt and pepper
- 12 small flour tortillas
- oil
- 2 avocados, diced
- 1/2 small red onion, diced
- 1 jalapeno, diced
- 4 tbsps cilantro, chopped
- 2 tsps lemon juice
- 1/2 C. cherry tomatoes, halved
- salt and pepper

Directions

- To make the taquitos:
- Get a large mixing bowl: Mix in it the chicken with lemon juice, cumin, jalapeno, cilantro, cheese, garlic, a pinch of salt and pepper. Place it aside to sit for 20 min.
- Lay a tortilla on a cookie sheet and place it in on the side of it in a long line 2 tbsps of the filling.

- Roll the tortilla over the filling in the shape of a cigar and place it in a lined up baking sheet. Repeat the process with remaining ingredients.
- Place a heavy pan over medium heat. Heat 1/4 inch of oil in it. Lay in it the taquitos gently and cook them for 2 to 4 min or until they become golden brown.
- Remove the taquitos from the hot oil and place them aside.
- To make the guacamole:
- Get a mixing bowl: Combine in it all the ingredients and mix them well. Serve your taquitos warm with the guacamole.
- Enjoy.

Servings Per Recipe: 1

Timing Information:

| Preparation | 15 mins |
| Total Time | 25 mins |

Nutritional Information:

Calories	228.0
Fat	11.0g
Cholesterol	30.4mg
Sodium	245.7mg
Carbohydrates	19.3g
Protein	13.2g

* Percent Daily Values are based on a 2,000 calorie diet.

Bolo de Biscoito de Limão

(Lime Biscuit Cake)

Ingredients

- 395 g sweetened condensed milk
- 300 ml cream
- 3 limes, juice and zest of
- 500 -750 g biscuits
- 1/2-1 C. milk

Directions

- Get a large mixing bowl: Combine in it the condensed milk with lime juice an cream. Use a hand mixer to beat them for 7 min until they become slightly thick.
- Get a shallow dish. Pour the milk in it. Lay the biscuits in the milk to coat them completely with it.
- Drain them and place 1/4 of them in the bottom of a serving glass dish. Pour over it 1/4 of the condensed mix.
- Repeat the process to make 3 more layers. Top your dessert with the lime zest and place it in the fridge for at least 2 h. serve it with your favorite toppings.
- Enjoy.

Servings Per Recipe: 12

Timing Information:

| Preparation | 15 mins |
| Total Time | 15 mins |

Nutritional Information:

Calories	336.0
Fat	17.9g
Cholesterol	42.1mg
Sodium	297.3mg
Carbohydrates	38.5g
Protein	6.4g

* Percent Daily Values are based on a 2,000 calorie diet.

Spicy Coconut Glazed Chicken

Ingredients

- 1 tsp ground cumin
- 1 tsp ground cayenne pepper
- 1 tsp ground turmeric
- 1 tsp ground coriander
- 4 boneless skinless chicken breast halves
- salt, to taste
- pepper, to taste
- 2 tbsps olive oil
- 1 onion, chopped
- 1 tbsp minced fresh ginger
- 2 jalapeno peppers, seeded and chopped
- 2 garlic cloves, minced
- 3 tomatoes, seeded and chopped
- 1 (14 oz.) cans light coconut milk
- 1 bunch chopped fresh parsley

Directions

- Get a small mixing bowl: Stir in it the cumin, cayenne pepper, turmeric, and coriander.
- Get a large mixing bowl: Sprinkle some salt and pepper over the chicken breasts then coat them with the spices mix.
- Place a large pan over medium heat and heat 1 tbsp of olive oil in it. Cook in it the chicken breasts for 14 to 16 min on each side or until they are done.
- Drain the breasts and place them aside. Add the onion, ginger, jalapeno peppers, and garlic to the same pan. Let them cook for 6 min.

- Stir in the tomato and cook them for an extra 7 min. Add the coconut milk with a pinch of salt and pepper. Cook them for 2 min.
- Serve your chicken breasts with your coconut sauce and enjoy.

Servings Per Recipe: 4

Timing Information:

| Preparation | 15 mins |
| Total Time | 1 hr |

Nutritional Information:

Calories	242.9
Fat	10.5g
Cholesterol	75.5mg
Sodium	158.7mg
Carbohydrates	10.0g
Protein	27.3g

* Percent Daily Values are based on a 2,000 calorie diet.

BRASILEIRO RICE

Ingredients

- 1/4 C. olive oil
- 2 onions, finely chopped
- 1 1/2 C. rice
- 3 C. hot chicken broth
- 10 oz. Italian plum tomatoes, canned drained and chopped
- salt, to taste
- cilantro, to garnish
- tomatoes, wedges to garnish

Directions

- Place a heavy saucepan over medium heat. Heat the oil in it. Cook in it the onion for 3 min.
- Stir in the rice and cook them for an extra 2 min. Stir in the broth, tomatoes, and salt. Cook them until they start boiling.
- Lower the heat and put on the lid. Cook the risotto for 22 min. Serve it warm.
- Enjoy.

Servings Per Recipe: 6

Timing Information:

| Preparation | 15 mins |
| Total Time | 40 mins |

Nutritional Information:

Calories	297.7
Fat	10.1g
Cholesterol	0.0mg
Sodium	377.8mg
Carbohydrates	44.4g
Protein	6.5g

* Percent Daily Values are based on a 2,000 calorie diet.

Easy Homemade Churrasco

Ingredients

- 2 lbs beef tenderloin
- 3 tsps salt
- 2 lemons, juice of
- 2 garlic cloves, mashed
- 1/4 tsp pepper
- 1/2 tsp crushed red pepper flakes
- 1 large onion, chopped
- 1/2 C. cilantro leaf

Directions

- Get a small mixing bowl: Mix in it the juice of 1 lemon, garlic, salt and pepper.
- Coat the tenderloin with the mix and wrap it with a piece of a plastic wrap. Place it in the fridge for an overnight.
- Preheat the grill and grease it.
- Drain the tenderloin with and grill until it is done to your liking.
- Get a small mixing bowl: Mix in it the rest of the lemon juice, onion, cilantro and pepper flakes to make the salsa.
- Serve your tenderloin warm with the onion salsa.
- Enjoy.

Servings Per Recipe: 4

Timing Information:

Preparation	20 mins
Total Time	1 hr

Nutritional Information:

Calories	583.8
Fat	41.3g
Cholesterol	192.7mg
Sodium	1860.5mg
Carbohydrates	5.8g
Protein	45.1g

* Percent Daily Values are based on a 2,000 calorie diet.

Brazilian Long Grain

Ingredients

- 1 large onion, peeled and cut into chunks
- 10 garlic cloves, peeled
- 1/2 C. fresh parsley leaves
- 1/2 C. fresh basil leaf
- 3 tbsps corn oil
- 2 C. long grain rice
- salt and pepper, to taste
- 3 C. chicken stock

Directions

- Get a food processor: Place in it the onion with garlic, parsley and basil. Process them until they become smooth.
- Place a heavy saucepan over medium heat. Heat the oil in it. Cook in it the rice for 3 min.
- Add 1 tbsp of the herbed onion mix with a pinch of salt and pepper. Cook them for 2 min.
- Stir in the stock and cook them until they start boiling. Put on the lid and let them cook for 18 to 22 min or until the rice is done.
- Fluff the rice with a fork. Add the remaining herbed onion mix and stir them to coat. Serve your warm salad.
- Enjoy.

Servings Per Recipe: 4

Timing Information:

| Preparation | 10 mins |
| Total Time | 30 mins |

Nutritional Information:

Calories	462.3
Fat	6.3g
Cholesterol	5.4mg
Sodium	269.2mg
Carbohydrates	86.9g
Protein	12.4g

* Percent Daily Values are based on a 2,000 calorie diet.

Bolo de Banana

Ingredients

- 3 tbsps margarine
- 2 C. white sugar
- 3 egg yolks
- 3 C. all-purpose flour
- 1 tbsp baking powder
- 1 C. milk
- 3 egg whites
- 6 bananas
- 2 tbsps white sugar
- 1 tsp ground cinnamon

Directions

- Before you do anything, preheat the oven to 350 F. Coat a baking pan with some butter.
- Get a large mixing bowl: Beat in it the sugar with butter until they become creamy.
- Add the egg yolks and beat them until they become smooth. Add the flour with baking powder and beat them again while adding the milk gradually until they become smooth.
- Place the egg whites in a large mixing bowl. Beat them until there soft peaks. Add it to the butter mix and stir them gently to fold them.
- Pour the batter in the greased pan and top it with the banana slices.
- Get a small mixing bowl: Mix in it the cinnamon with 2 tbsps of sugar. Sprinkle the mix over the banana slices.
- Cook it in the oven for 34 to 36 min. Allow the cake to cool down completely. Serve it with your favorite toppings.

Servings Per Recipe: 12

Timing Information:

| Preparation | 25 mins |
| Total Time | 1 hr |

Nutritional Information:

Calories	359.4
Fat	5.1g
Cholesterol	50.0mg
Sodium	150.7mg
Carbohydrates	74.3g
Protein	6.0g

* Percent Daily Values are based on a 2,000 calorie diet.

Brazilian Lunch Special

(Black Beans with Chicken)

Ingredients

- 1 (8 oz.) packages Mexican-style chicken rice pilaf mix
- 1 (16 oz.) cans black beans, rinsed and drained
- 1 C. corn, canned or frozen
- 1 bunch scallion, chopped
- 1/2 C. pitted black olives, sliced lengthwise
- 4 C. cooked diced chicken meat
- 1/2 bunch fresh cilantro, chopped
- 1 ripe avocado, sliced
- salsa
- sour cream
- tortilla chips

Directions

- Cook the rice by following the directions on the package. Fluff it with a fork.
- Stir into it the black beans, corn, scallions, olives, chicken and cilantro. Serve your salad with your favorite toppings.
- Enjoy.

Servings Per Recipe: 4

Timing Information:

Preparation	5 mins
Total Time	40 mins

Nutritional Information:

Calories	258.8
Fat	10.2g
Cholesterol	0.0mg
Sodium	137.1mg
Carbohydrates	36.0g
Protein	10.5g

* Percent Daily Values are based on a 2,000 calorie diet.

3-Ingredient Sun Salad

Ingredients

- 5 oranges
- 1 tsp sugar
- salt and pepper

Directions

- Discard the oranges peel and white pith.
- Slice the oranges thinly and place them on a serving plate.
- Top them with sugar, a pinch of salt and pepper. Place the salad in the fridge until ready to serve.
- Enjoy.

Servings Per Recipe: 5

Timing Information:

Preparation	10 mins
Total Time	10 mins

Nutritional Information:

Calories	64.8
Fat	0.1g
Cholesterol	0.0mg
Sodium	0.0mg
Carbohydrates	16.2g
Protein	1.2g

* Percent Daily Values are based on a 2,000 calorie diet.

Cod and Coconut Stew

Ingredients

- 1 lb fresh cod
- 2 limes, juice of
- 1 tsp salt
- 2 tbsps oil
- 2 onions, diced
- 1 bell pepper, diced (any color)
- 3 garlic cloves, minced
- 6 tomatoes, peeled seeded, diced
- 2 C. coconut milk
- 1 tsp Old Bay Seasoning
- pepper

Directions

- Get a large mixing bowl: Whisk in it the juice of 2 limes with a pinch of salt. Dip in it the cod fish and cover it with a plastic wrap. Place it in the fridge for 32 min.
- Place a large saucepan over medium heat. Heat the oil in it. Add the peppers with onion and cook them for 2 min. Stir in the garlic and cook them for 60 min.
- Stir in the tomato and cook them for 12 min. Add the fish with the coconut milk and old bay seasoning. Cook them until they start boiling.
- Lower the heat and cook the stew for 12 min. Serve it hot.
- Enjoy.

Servings Per Recipe: 2

Timing Information:

| Preparation | 15 mins |
| Total Time | 30 mins |

Nutritional Information:

Calories	1015.1
Fat	68.5g
Cholesterol	97.4mg
Sodium	1458.1mg
Carbohydrates	57.7g
Protein	53.5g

* Percent Daily Values are based on a 2,000 calorie diet.

Sao Paulo Poundcake

Ingredients

- 1/2 C. brazil nut
- 1/4 lb unsalted butter, softened
- 6 tbsps brown sugar, packed
- 3/4 C. flour
- 3 tbsps rice flour
- 1/2 tsp cinnamon

Directions

- Before you do anything preheat the oven to 325 F.
- Get a food processor: place in it the nuts and process them until they become finely ground.
- Get a mixing bowl: Beat in it the sugar with butter until they become light and fluffy.
- Add to them the ground nuts with flour and mix them well. Transfer the dough to a lined up baking sheet.
- Flatten it slightly with a rolling pin then use a sharp knife to prick on the sides to make 8 wedges without cutting them.
- Top the dough circle with some granulated sugar and cook it in the oven for 42 min.
- Allow your giant cookie to cool down completely then serve it.
- Enjoy.

Servings Per Recipe: 1

Timing Information:

Preparation	15 mins
Total Time	1 hr 15 mins

Nutritional Information:

Calories	254.7
Fat	17.4g
Cholesterol	30.5mg
Sodium	6.1mg
Carbohydrates	23.1g
Protein	2.8g

* Percent Daily Values are based on a 2,000 calorie diet.

Sweet and Salty Raisin Rice

Ingredients

Rice

- 1 1/2 C. long-grain white rice
- 2 1/2 C. water (or more)
- 1/2 tsp salt
- 1 tbsp butter, unsalted

Spice

- 1 tbsp olive oil
- 3 slices turkey bacon, cut into strips
- 1/2 medium red onion, diced
- 1 garlic clove, peeled and minced
- 1/2 green bell pepper, diced
- 1/2 red bell pepper, diced
- 1/2 C. corn kernel, cooked
- 1/4 C. raisins, dark
- 1/4 C. raisins, golden
- 3 tbsps Italian parsley, chopped
- salt & pepper, to taste

Directions

- Place a large pot over medium heat. Rinse the rice and place it in it then add to it 2 1/2 C. of water.

- Add to it some butter with a pinch of salt. Cook it until it starts boiling. Put n the lid and lower the heat then let it cook for 22 min.
- Turn off the heat and let the rice rest for 6 min. Use a fork to fluff it and place it aside.
- Place a large skillet over medium heat. Heat the oil in it. Brown in it the bacon for 5 min. Drain it and place it aside.
- Reserve 2 tbsps of bacon fat in the skillet and discard the remaining of it. Stir in the onion, garlic, bell peppers, corn, both raisins, and the parsley.
- Let them cook for 6 min while stirring them from time to time. Add the rice and cook them for an extra 2 min.
- Adjust the seasoning of your rice skillet then serve it warm.
- Enjoy.

Servings Per Recipe: 4

Timing Information:

Preparation	15 mins
Total Time	45 mins

Nutritional Information:

Calories	441.7
Fat	9.9g
Cholesterol	11.7mg
Sodium	380.5mg
Carbohydrates	81.7g
Protein	8.0g

* Percent Daily Values are based on a 2,000 calorie diet.

Classic Dry Beef Chuck and Coconut Stew

Ingredients

- 3 lbs beef chuck, cut into 1 inch cubes
- 4 tbsps olive oil
- 6 large tomatoes, cut into wedges
- 1 large yellow onion, chopped
- 3 garlic cloves, minced
- 2 tsps fresh ginger, grated
- 1 (13 1/2 oz.) cans unsweetened coconut milk
- 1 tbsp dried oregano
- 1 tbsp red pepper flakes
- 1 tsp salt
- 1 tsp pepper
- 1 (19 oz.) cans black beans, drained and rinsed
- 1/3 C. fresh cilantro, chopped

Directions

- Place a large pan over high heat. Heat in it the olive oil. Brown in it the beef in batches for 5 min per batch.
- Stir the tomatoes, onion, garlic and ginger and cook them for 4 min. Add the coconut milk with oregano, red pepper flakes, salt and pepper.

- Cook them until they start boiling. Put on the lid and let them cook for 1 h 32 min while stirring them from time to time.
- Add the beans to the stew and let them cook for an extra 16 min. Adjust the seasoning of the stew and serve it warm.
- Enjoy.

Servings Per Recipe: 4

Timing Information:

| Preparation | 20 mins |
| Total Time | 2 hrs 20 mins |

Nutritional Information:

Calories	1386.4
Fat	102.6g
Cholesterol	234.7mg
Sodium	812.6mg
Carbohydrates	42.5g
Protein	76.3g

* Percent Daily Values are based on a 2,000 calorie diet.

South American Seafood Soup

Ingredients

- 1 lb shrimp, peeled and veined
- 1/4 lb bay scallop
- 6 oz. white fish fillets, (cod fillet)
- 2 garlic cloves, minced
- 1/4 C. lemon juice
- 1 1/2 tsps salt
- 1/2 tsp black pepper
- 2 C. tomatoes, with juice
- 3/4 C. white onion
- 2 -3 limes, to make 1/4 c juice plus
- 1/2 C. red pepper, diced
- 1/2 C. green pepper, diced
- 1 jalapeno, seeded, diced
- 2 tbsps olive oil
- 1 (6 oz.) cans tomato paste
- 1/2 C. cilantro, chopped, divided
- 2 tsps fresh gingerroot
- 1/2 tsp crushed red pepper flakes (to taste)
- 1/4 tsp ground cayenne pepper
- 13 1/2 oz. unsweetened coconut milk

Directions

- Get a large mixing bowl: Stir in it the shrimp, scallops, fish ,garlic, lemon juice, 1/2 tsp salt and black pepper.
- Cover it with a plastic wrap and place it in the fridge for 22 min.

- Get a food processor: Combine in it the canned tomatoes with juices, 1/2 of cilantro, onions, jalapeno and 1/4 c lime juice. Blend them smooth and place it aside.
- Place a large pot over medium heat. Heat the oil in it. Sauté in it the red and green pepper with pepper flakes for 9 min.
- Add the rest of the cilantro, ginger, cayenne, and remaining salt. Sauté them for 1 min while stirring all the time.
- Stir in the tomato mix and cook them until they start boiling. Let them cook for 16 min over low heat.
- Add the tomato paste with coconut milk and bring them to another boil. Stir in the seafood and cook them again until they start boiling.
- Let the stew cook for 6 min. Adjust the seasoning of the stew then serve it warm.
- Enjoy.

Servings Per Recipe: 4

Timing Information:

Preparation	20 mins
Total Time	55 mins

Nutritional Information:

Calories	479.0
Fat	29.6g
Cholesterol	178.4mg
Sodium	2016.7mg
Carbohydrates	26.8g
Protein	32.4g

* Percent Daily Values are based on a 2,000 calorie diet.

Rice Skillet with Orange and Pimento

Ingredients

- 1 lb boneless chicken thighs, skinless, cut into 1/2 inch wide strips
- 1/4 C. olive oil
- 4 garlic cloves, finely chopped
- 1 tsp orange zest
- 1 1/2 C. water
- 1/2 C. orange juice
- 1 (8 oz.) packages yellow rice mix
- 1/2 C. pimento stuffed olive, halves
- 1 C. fresh cilantro, chopped
- orange wedge (to garnish)

Directions

- Season the chicken strips with a pinch of salt and pepper.
- Place a large pan over medium heat. Heat the oil in it. Brown in it the chicken with garlic and zest. Cook them for 4 min.
- Stir in 1 1/2 C. water and 1/2 C. orange juice. Cook them until they start boiling. Stir in the rice with seasoning packet, and olives.
- Cook them until they start boiling. Lower the heat and put on the lid. Let them cook for 20 min. Once the time is up, serve your chicken and rice skillet hot.
- Enjoy.

Servings Per Recipe: 4

Timing Information:

| Preparation | 20 mins |
| Total Time | 50 mins |

Nutritional Information:

Calories	378.6
Fat	30.9g
Cholesterol	95.3mg
Sodium	91.8mg
Carbohydrates	4.4g
Protein	20.1g

* Percent Daily Values are based on a 2,000 calorie diet.

Brazilian Vegetarian Hot Pot) (Ginger and Coconut Curry

Ingredients

- 1 butternut squash, peeled and 2 cm dice
- 2 red onions, roughly chopped
- 1 aubergine, chopped
- 2 red peppers, diced
- 1 (400 g) cans chickpeas
- 2 garlic cloves, crushed
- 1/2 inch gingerroot, chopped
- 1 red chili pepper, deseeded and chopped
- 400 g chopped tomatoes
- 200 ml coconut cream
- 4 tbsps chopped fresh coriander
- 3 tbsps olive oil

Directions

- Before you do anything preheat the oven to 400 F.
- Get a large mixing bowl: Mix in it the veggies with 2 tbsps of oil. Spread the mix on a baking sheet and cook it for 42 min in the oven.
- Get a blender: Combine in it the chili, garlic, ginger and onion. Blend them smooth.
- Place a large pot over medium heat. Heat the rest of oil in it. Sauté in it the onion mix for 2 min. Stir in the tomato and cook it for 12 min.

- Stir in the coconut cream and let them cook for 6 min. Once the time is up, stir in the roasted veggies.
- Serve your curry hot.
- Enjoy.

Servings Per Recipe: 6

Timing Information:

| Preparation | 15 mins |
| Total Time | 1 hr |

Nutritional Information:

Calories	432.8
Fat	14.8g
Cholesterol	0.0mg
Sodium	230.9mg
Carbohydrates	72.8g
Protein	8.0g

* Percent Daily Values are based on a 2,000 calorie diet.

Black Bean Stew I

Ingredients

- 1 tbsp olive oil
- 1 stalk celery, small dice
- 2 carrots, peeled and small dice
- 2 medium onions, peeled and small dice
- 3 garlic cloves, peeled and minced
- 1 small red bell pepper, seeded and small dice
- 1 lb lean stewing beef, cut into 1/2 inch cubes
- 1 tsp ground cumin
- 1 tsp orange zest, Grated
- 1 (14 1/2 oz.) cans diced tomatoes, undrained
- 2 (14 1/2 oz.) cans black beans, drained and rinsed
- salt and pepper, to taste

Directions

- Place a large pot over medium heat. Heat the oil in it. Cook in it the celery, carrots, onions, garlic, and bell pepper with the lid on for 6 min.
- Stir in the cumin, orange zest and tomatoes. Let them cook for 32 min over low heat with the lid on.
- Once the time is up, add the black beans to pot. Let them cook for 28 min without covering the pot. Adjust the seasoning of the soup then serve it hot.
- Enjoy.

Servings Per Recipe: 6

Timing Information:

| Preparation | 20 mins |
| Total Time | 1 hr 24 mins |

Nutritional Information:

Calories	340.0
Fat	11.8g
Cholesterol	55.2mg
Sodium	69.0mg
Carbohydrates	33.1g
Protein	25.9g

* Percent Daily Values are based on a 2,000 calorie diet.

Steak with Chimichurri

Ingredients

Chimichurri

- 1 bunch flat leaf parsley, leaves only
- 3 garlic cloves, peeled
- 3 tbsps red wine vinegar
- 1/2 lime, juice of, only
- 3 tbsps chopped oregano leaves
- 1 tsp ground cumin

Steak

- 1 tsp smoked paprika
- 120 ml extra virgin olive oil
- 1 red chili pepper, halved and seeded
- 1 (200 g) rib eye steaks
- 1 tbsp oil
- 1 bunch watercress
- cooked potato, sautéed with
- ground cumin

Directions

- To make the chimichurri:
- Get a blender: Combine in it all the chimichurri and blend them smooth. Adjust the seasoning of the sauce and place it aside.
- To make the rib eye steak:
- Coat the whole steak with oil then sprinkle over it some salt and pepper.
- Place a griddle pan over medium heat. Cook in it the steak for 2 to 4 min on each side.

- Serve your steak with watercress, potato, a pinch of cumin and the chimichurri sauce.
- Enjoy.

Servings Per Recipe: 1

Timing Information:

| Preparation | 10 mins |
| Total Time | 30 mins |

Nutritional Information:

Calories	1690.7
Fat	163.7g
Cholesterol	136.0mg
Sodium	202.2mg
Carbohydrates	20.6g
Protein	41.7g

* Percent Daily Values are based on a 2,000 calorie diet.

Fortaleza Stroganoff

Ingredients

- 2 lbs beef or 2 lbs chicken fillets, cut into 1 inch pieces
- 2 garlic cloves, minced
- 1 onion, chopped, divided
- salt
- 1/4 tsp nutmeg
- 1/2 tsp oregano
- 1/2 C. dry white wine
- 2 tbsps oil
- 1/2 lb cultivated white mushroom, sliced
- 2 -3 tbsps ketchup
- 1 1/2 tbsps mild mustard
- 1/2 C. sour cream

Directions

- Get a large mixing bowl: Combine in it the meat with garlic, half the onion, salt, nutmeg, oregano and wine. Toss them to coat. Let them sit for 1 h.
- Place a large skillet over medium heat. Heat the oil in it. Combine in it the rest of the onion with mushroom. Cook them for 4 min.
- Stir in the meat mix with mustard, ketchup and few tbsps of water. Let them cook for 8 to 12 min or until the meat is done.
- Once the time is up, stir in the cream. Heat the stew for 2 min then serve it hot.
- Enjoy.

Servings Per Recipe: 4

Timing Information:

Preparation	30 mins
Total Time	50 mins

Nutritional Information:

Calories	1707.3
Fat	173.9g
Cholesterol	239.6mg
Sodium	235.1mg
Carbohydrates	8.8g
Protein	21.8g

* Percent Daily Values are based on a 2,000 calorie diet.

Eveline's Latin Lasagna

Ingredients

- 2 tbsps butter
- 3 tbsps all-purpose flour
- 1 C. milk
- 1/4 tsp nutmeg
- 1 tsp salt
- 1/4 tsp ground black pepper
- 2 tbsps vegetable oil
- 1 small white onion, chopped
- 1 garlic clove, crushed
- 1/2 lb ground beef
- 1 lb ripe tomatoes, peeled, seeds removed, and chopped
- 1 lb uncooked lasagna noodles
- 1/2 lb sliced mozzarella cheese
- 1/2 lb thinly sliced ham, optional
- 2 oz. grated parmesan cheese
- 2 tsps oregano
- 2 tsps salt

Directions

- Before you do anything, preheat the oven to 350 F.
- Place a large saucepan over medium heat. Melt the butter in it. Stir in the nutmeg with a pinch of salt and pepper.
- Stir in the milk and cook them until it starts boiling. let it cook for 12 min to make the white sauce.
- Place a large saucepan over medium high heat. Heat the vegetable oil in it. Cook in it the beef, onion and garlic for 8 min.

- Stir in the water with tomato and cook them for 6 to 8 min or until the sauce becomes thick.
- Prepare the noodles according to the instructions on the package. Drain it and place 1/4 of it in the bottom of a grease casserole dish.
- Spread over it 1/2 of the meat sauce then cover it with 1/4 of the noodles. Top it with half of the cheese and ham then repeat the process to make 2 more layers.
- Pour the white sauce on top followed by the parmesan cheese and a pinch of oregano. Lay a piece of foil over the lasagna casserole to cover it.
- Cook it in the oven for 22 min. Serve your lasagna hot.
- Enjoy.

Servings Per Recipe: 4

Timing Information:

| Preparation | 30 mins |
| Total Time | 50 mins |

Nutritional Information:

Calories	1075.4
Fat	48.7g
Cholesterol	245.0mg
Sodium	3327.1mg
Carbohydrates	96.8g
Protein	61.3g

* Percent Daily Values are based on a 2,000 calorie diet.

Coconut Shrimp Pot

Ingredients

- 1 1/4 lbs large shrimp
- 1 1/2 tsps salt
- 1/4 tsp pepper
- 2 garlic cloves, minced
- 1/4 C. fresh lemon juice
- 1 (14 oz.) cans diced tomatoes, with juice
- 1 medium onion, finely chopped
- 1 green pepper, finely chopped
- 1 1/2 tbsps oil
- 1/2 tsp cayenne
- 5 tbsps coarsely chopped cilantro
- 1 C. coconut milk, well stirred
- 1 tbsp palm oil

Directions

- Get a large mixing bowl: Combine in it the shrimp with garlic, 1/2 tsp salt and pepper and lemon juice. Place in the fridge for 20 min at least.
- Get a food processor: Place in it the tomato and blend it smooth.
- Place a pot over medium heat. Heat the olive oil in it. Sauté in it the bell pepper with onion for 9 to 11 min.
- Add the cayenne pepper with cilantro and a pinch of salt. Cook them for 1 extra min.
- Stir in the tomato and let them cook for 16 min over low heat. Add the coconut milk and cook them until they start boiling.

- Stir in the shrimp mix and let them cook for 4 to 6 min. Stir in the palm oil then serve your stew warm.
- Enjoy.

Servings Per Recipe: 6

Timing Information:

| Preparation | 25 mins |
| Total Time | 45 mins |

Nutritional Information:

Calories	219.4
Fat	14.9g
Cholesterol	119.3mg
Sodium	1127.8mg
Carbohydrates	8.3g
Protein	14.7g

* Percent Daily Values are based on a 2,000 calorie diet.

Mushrooms Brasileiro

Ingredients

- 4 mushrooms, flat large, stalks trimmed, sliced into quarters
- 2 garlic cloves, crushed
- 1 small lime, juice of
- 2 tbsps extra virgin olive oil
- salt and pepper

Spice Mix

- 1/2 tsp paprika
- 1/2 tsp cumin
- 1/2 tsp coriander, ground seed
- 1/2 tsp dried chili, flakes
- 1/4 tsp allspice

Directions

- Get a small mixing bowl: Combine in it the spice ingredients.
- Get a large mixing bowl: Toss in it the mushrooms, garlic, lime juice and olive oil. Add the spice mix and toss them to coat. Let them sit for 12 min.
- Before you do anything preheat the grill.
- Grease the grill and cook in it the mushroom for 2 to 4 min on each side. Serve them hot.
- Enjoy.

Servings Per Recipe: 4

Timing Information:

Preparation	40 mins
Total Time	50 mins

Nutritional Information:

Calories	73.3
Fat	6.9g
Cholesterol	0.0mg
Sodium	2.4mg
Carbohydrates	3.2g
Protein	0.8g

* Percent Daily Values are based on a 2,000 calorie diet.

Bananas Assadas Quentes

Ingredients

- 3 tbsps butter, cut into small pieces
- 1/2 C. firmly packed brown sugar
- 1 tbsp lemon juice
- 2 medium bananas, firm and ripe
- 2 cinnamon sticks
- rind of one lime, cut into thin strips
- 1/3 C. sweetened flaked coconut

Directions

- Get a shallow microwave safe bowl: Combine in it the butter, brown sugar and lemon juice. Microwave them for 60 sec on high.
- Discard the banana peel and slice them in half crosswise. Cut each slice in half lengthwise.
- Dip the banana pieces in the sugar and lemon mix. Place the banana slices on a lined up baking sheet. Top them with the lime peel and cinnamon sticks.
- Microwave them for 120 sec on high. Coat the banana pieces another time with the sugar sauce. Cook them again in the microwave for 120 sec.
- Roll the banana pops in the coconut flakes then serve them with the remaining sauce.
- Enjoy.

Servings Per Recipe: 4

Timing Information:

Preparation	10 mins
Total Time	16 mins

Nutritional Information:

Calories	273.0
Fat	11.5g
Cholesterol	22.9mg
Sodium	104.6mg
Carbohydrates	44.4g
Protein	1.0g

* Percent Daily Values are based on a 2,000 calorie diet.

Tropical Mango Stew

Ingredients

- 1/2 tbsp canola oil
- 1 small onion, chopped
- 1 garlic clove, minced
- 1 medium sweet potato, peeled and diced
- 1 small red bell pepper, diced
- 3/4 lb tomatoes, diced
- 3/4 C. water
- 1 (16 oz.) cans black beans, well-rinsed and drained
- 1 mango, peeled, seeded and diced
- 1/8 C. chopped fresh cilantro
- salt, to taste (optional)

Directions

- Place a large saucepan over medium heat. Heat the oil in it. Sauté in it the garlic with onion for 3 min.
- Stir in the sweet potato, bell pepper, tomatoes, and water. Cook them until they start boiling. Lower the heat and put on the lid. Cook them for 16 min.
- Stir in the beans and cook the stew for 5 min. Stir in the mango and cilantro and pinch of salt to taste. Serve your stew warm.
- Enjoy.

Servings Per Recipe: 4

Timing Information:

Preparation	10 mins
Total Time	40 mins

Nutritional Information:

Calories	226.2
Fat	2.7g
Cholesterol	0.0mg
Sodium	25.1mg
Carbohydrates	43.9g
Protein	9.4g

* Percent Daily Values are based on a 2,000 calorie diet.

Ensalada de Papas I

Ingredients

- 2 lbs sweet potatoes
- 1 tbsp salt
- 1/2 C. drained and rinsed black beans
- 1/2 red onion, chopped
- 1/4 C. fresh cilantro, chopped

Sauce

- 1/2 C. mayonnaise
- 2 tbsps olive oil
- 1 tsp Dijon mustard
- 1 tsp Worcestershire sauce
- 2 tbsps red wine vinegar
- 1/2 tsp salt
- 1/2 tsp pepper

Directions

- Cut off the top and ends of the potato and rinse them. Place them in a large pot and pour on them enough water to cover them.
- Stir in 1 tbsp of salt and put on the lid. Cook them until they start boiling. Let them cook for 25 to 30 until the potato is tender.
- Discard the potato skin and cut it into dices.
- Get a large mixing bowl: Mix in it the mayonnaise, olive oil, Dijon mustard, Worcestershire sauce, red wine vinegar, 1/2 tsp salt and pepper.
- Add to them the potato with black beans, onion and cilantro. Stir them well to coat. Place the salad in the fridge until ready to serve.

Servings Per Recipe: 6

Timing Information:

| Preparation | 15 mins |
| Total Time | 45 mins |

Nutritional Information:

Calories	271.7
Fat	11.2g
Cholesterol	5.0mg
Sodium	1599.0mg
Carbohydrates	39.7g
Protein	4.0g

* Percent Daily Values are based on a 2,000 calorie diet.

How to Roast Brazilian Nuts

Ingredients

- 1 lb brazil nut
- 2 tbsps olive oil
- salt

Directions

- Before you do anything, preheat the oven broiler.
- Place the nuts on a lined up baking sheet. Pour over them 2 tbsps of olive oil and toss them to coat.
- Roast the nuts in the oven for 3 to 4 min. Pat the nuts dry and season them with some salt. Serve your toasted Brazilian nuts.
- Enjoy.

Servings Per Recipe: 1

Timing Information:

Preparation	5 mins
Total Time	8 mins

Nutritional Information:

Calories	3214.3
Fat	328.3g
Cholesterol	0.0mg
Sodium	14.1mg
Carbohydrates	55.6g
Protein	64.9g

* Percent Daily Values are based on a 2,000 calorie diet.

Onion Salad South American

Ingredients

- 2 large onions
- 2 tbsps sugar
- 1 tbsp red wine vinegar
- 2 tbsps olive oil
- salt
- pepper

Directions

- Discard the onion skin and thinly slice it.
- Get a large mixing bowl: Fill it with some ice and water. Place in it the onion rings and let it sit in the fridge for 2 h.
- Drain the onion rings and run them under some cool water. Place them in a serving bowl.
- Top them with the extra-virgin olive oil and red wine vinegar, and a pinch of salt and freshly ground pepper. Serve it right away.
- Enjoy.

Servings Per Recipe: 4

Timing Information:

Preparation	10 mins
Total Time	2 hrs 10 mins

Nutritional Information:

Calories	114.7
Fat	6.8g
Cholesterol	0.0mg
Sodium	3.5mg
Carbohydrates	13.3g
Protein	0.8g

* Percent Daily Values are based on a 2,000 calorie diet.

Chipotle Beans Stew with Rice

Ingredients

- 5 1/2 C. dried black beans, rinsed and drained
- 1 tbsp canola oil
- 1 large yellow onion, diced
- 2 medium red bell peppers
- 1 large tomatoes, diced
- 4 garlic cloves, minced
- 1 canned chipotle pepper, chopped
- 2 C. sweet potatoes, peeled and diced
- 2 tsps dried thyme leaves
- 2 tsps dried parsley
- 1 tsp salt
- 4 C. cooked rice

Directions

- Place a large pot over medium heat. Put in it the beans and cover it with water. Put on the lid and let it cook for 60 min.
- Once the time is up, drain the beans and reserve 2 C. of the beans cooking liquid.
- Place a pot over medium heat. Heat the oil in it. Sauté in it the onion, bell peppers, tomato, garlic, and chipotle peppers for 9 to 11 min.

- Stir in the beans, cooking liquid, sweet potatoes, and thyme. Let them cook for 28 to 32 min.
- Once the time is up, add the parsley with a pinch of salt to the stew. Let it cook for 8 min. serve it hot with some rice.
- Enjoy.

Servings Per Recipe: 6

Timing Information:

| Preparation | 1 h |
| Total Time | 2 h |

Nutritional Information:

Calories	858.1
Fat	5.3g
Cholesterol	0.0mg
Sodium	426.1mg
Carbohydrates	162.0g
Protein	43.1g

* Percent Daily Values are based on a 2,000 calorie diet.

Salvador Chicken Stew

Ingredients

- 1 tsp olive oil
- 4 C. boneless skinless chicken breasts
- 1 large onion, sliced
- 1 1/2 green bell pepper, diced
- 1 red bell pepper, diced
- 3 garlic cloves, chopped
- 1/2 bay leaf
- 1 tsp garlic powder
- 1/4 tsp cumin
- 1/4 tsp dried oregano
- 5 (8 oz.) cans no-salt-added tomato sauce
- 2 1/2 C. water
- 1 tbsp fresh lemon juice
- 4 C. celery, chopped

Directions

- Place a large pot over medium heat. Heat 1 tsp of oil in it. Sauté in it the chicken pieces for 3 min.
- Stir in the onions, peppers and garlic. Cook them for 4 min.
- Stir in the tomato sauce, water, bay leaf, garlic powder, cumin and oregano. Cook them until they start boiling. Lower the heat and cook them stew for 1 h 45 min.

- Discard the bay leaf. Serve your stew hot.
- Enjoy.

Servings Per Recipe: 6

Timing Information:

| Preparation | 15 mins |
| Total Time | 2 hrs 30 mins |

Nutritional Information:

Calories	112.4
Fat	1.4g
Cholesterol	0.0mg
Sodium	79.2mg
Carbohydrates	22.2g
Protein	3.8g

* Percent Daily Values are based on a 2,000 calorie diet.

Brazilian Sausage

Ingredients

- 1 1/2 lbs linguica sausage
- 6 oz. coarsely grated cheese

Directions

- Before you do anything, preheat the grill and grease it.
- Cut each sausage in a half lengthwise. Grill the sausage slices for 4 min on each side.
- Adjust the sausages halves to make their open side facing up. Top them with the grated cheese and cook them for 4 min.
- Serve your cheesy sausages hot.
- Enjoy.

Servings Per Recipe: 8

Timing Information:

Preparation	0 mins
Total Time	10 mins

Nutritional Information:

Calories	70.5
Fat	5.2g
Cholesterol	13.6mg
Sodium	205.7mg
Carbohydrates	1.7g
Protein	4.1g

* Percent Daily Values are based on a 2,000 calorie diet.

Spicy Pink Shrimp

Ingredients

- 1 1/2 lbs raw shrimp, peeled & deveined
- 1/4 C. olive oil
- 1/4 C. onion, diced
- 1 garlic clove, minced
- 1/4 C. roasted red pepper, diced
- 1/4 C. fresh cilantro, chopped
- 14 oz. diced tomatoes
- 1 C. coconut milk
- 2 tbsps sriracha sauce
- 2 tbsps fresh lime juice
- salt and pepper

Directions

- Place a large saucepan over medium heat. Heat the oil in it.
- Cook in it the onion for 3 min. Stir in the garlic with peppers for another 3 min.
- Stir in the tomatoes, shrimp and cilantro. Cook them for 4 min.
- Stir in the coconut milk and Sriracha sauce. Cook them for 3 min. Stir in the lime juice with a pinch of salt and pepper. Serve your stew warm.
- Enjoy.

Servings Per Recipe: 6

Timing Information:

Preparation	20 mins
Total Time	50 mins

Nutritional Information:

Calories	352.1
Fat	18.2g
Cholesterol	143.2mg
Sodium	1007.2mg
Carbohydrates	31.1g
Protein	16.6g

* Percent Daily Values are based on a 2,000 calorie diet.

Potato Salad Brazilian II

Ingredients

- 5 -6 medium white rose potatoes
- 1 medium apple, peeled cored and finely diced
- 1 C. carrot, cooked till tender but not mushy, diced into small cubes
- 1 C. frozen peas, lightly blanched and cooled
- 1 C. frozen corn kernels, defrosted
- 1 C. mayonnaise, to taste
- 1/2 C. sliced pimento-stuffed green olives
- salt and pepper, to taste

Directions

- Get a large mixing bowl: Mix in it all the ingredients.
- Adjust the seasoning of the salad and serve it right away.
- Enjoy.

Servings Per Recipe: 10

Timing Information:

Preparation	20 mins
Total Time	20 mins

Nutritional Information:

Calories	211.8
Fat	8.1g
Cholesterol	6.1mg
Sodium	197.9mg
Carbohydrates	32.8g
Protein	3.7g

* Percent Daily Values are based on a 2,000 calorie diet.

BRASILEIRO SKIRTS

Ingredients

- 1 whole skirt steak
- sea salt (enough to coat steak)

Directions

- Season the steak with some salt on both sides.
- Place a pan over medium high heat. Grease it and cook in it the steak for 2 to 4 mi on each.
- You can grill it also or bake it for 26 min on 350 F. Serve it warm.
- Enjoy.

Servings Per Recipe: 2

Timing Information:

Preparation	8 mins
Total Time	48 mins

Nutritional Information:

Calories	371.9
Fat	18.6g
Cholesterol	147.4mg
Sodium	151.9mg
Carbohydrates	0.0g
Protein	47.8g

* Percent Daily Values are based on a 2,000 calorie diet.

AMBROSIA PUDDING

Ingredients

- 6 eggs
- 1/2 C. orange juice
- 2 tbsps orange zest, grated
- 1/2 lb sugar

Directions

- Before you do anything, preheat the oven to 300 F.
- Get a mixing bowl: Whisk in it all the ingredients. Pour the mix through a fine mesh sieve to strain it.
- Pour the batter in a greased 8/6 inches ceramic dish. Cook the pudding in the oven for 22 min. serve it with your favorite toppings after it cools down.
- Enjoy.

Servings Per Recipe: 4

Timing Information:

| Preparation | 10 mins |
| Total Time | 30 mins |

Nutritional Information:

Calories	343.5
Fat	7.2g
Cholesterol	279.0mg
Sodium	107.4mg
Carbohydrates	61.2g
Protein	9.6g

* Percent Daily Values are based on a 2,000 calorie diet.

Habanero Rice

Ingredients

- 1 tbsp vegetable oil
- 1 small onion, finely diced
- 1 garlic clove, minced
- 1 C. long-grain rice
- 1 habanero pepper
- 2 -2 1/4 C. hot water
- 1/2 tsp salt

Directions

- Place a pot over medium heat. Heat the oil in it. Cook in it the rice with garlic and onion for 5 min.
- Stir in the chili pepper, hot water, and salt. Cook them until they start boiling.
- Let the rice cook for 18 to 22 min or until the rice is done. Let it sit for 5 min the fluff it with a fork.
- Discard the hot pepper and serve your rice warm.
- Enjoy.

Servings Per Recipe: 4

Timing Information:

Preparation	5 mins
Total Time	35 mins

Nutritional Information:

Calories	211.4
Fat	3.7g
Cholesterol	0.0mg
Sodium	298.3mg
Carbohydrates	39.8g
Protein	3.7g

* Percent Daily Values are based on a 2,000 calorie diet.

Feijoada II

(Full Black Bean Stew)

Ingredients

- 1 1/2 lbs small black turtle beans, soaked for an overnight
- 1/2 lb brazilian dried beef
- 1 ham hock
- 1 lb pork ribs
- 1 lb smoked chorizo sausage
- 1 lb beef sirloin
- 1/2 lb slab smoked bacon
- 1/2 lb smoked pig (optional)
- 1/4 C. vegetable oil
- 2 onions, finely chopped
- 3 garlic cloves, mashed
- 1/3 C. parsley, chopped
- 1 1/2 tsps cumin
- 1 bay leaf
- salt and pepper, to taste

Directions

- Place a large pot over medium heat. place in it the beans and cover it with water.
- Stir in the ham hock with dry beef. Cook them for 2 h. Once the time is up, discard the ham hock.
- Add the smoked bacon with sirloin, pork ribs, and bay leaf to the beans pot. Let them cook for 32 min.

- Place a large pan over medium heat. Heat the oil in it. Sauté in it the garlic with onion for 3 min.
- Stir in the parsley with cumin, a pinch of salt and pepper. Cook them for 1 min.
- Stir in 3/4 C. of beans mix and mash them with a fork. Pour the mix into the beans pot and cook them for an extra 30 min.
- Drain the meats and slice them then place them on a serving plate. Drain the beans serve it with some white rice along with the meats.
- Enjoy.

Servings Per Recipe: 8

Timing Information:

Preparation	15 hrs
Total Time	18 hrs

Nutritional Information:

Calories	2536.5
Fat	170.5g
Cholesterol	834.8mg
Sodium	2651.0mg
Carbohydrates	5.5g
Protein	230.6g

* Percent Daily Values are based on a 2,000 calorie diet.

Brasileiro Flank

Ingredients

- 2 lbs flank steaks
- 6 garlic cloves, minced
- 1/2 small hot pepper
- 2 tsp extra virgin olive oil
- 1/4 tsp kosher salt
- 1 (14 oz) cans hearts of palm, drained, halved lengthwise and thinly sliced
- 4 medium tomatoes, chopped
- 1/2 C. red onion, chopped
- 1/2 small hot chili peppers
- 1/4 C. fresh cilantro, chopped
- 2 tbsp red wine vinegar
- 1/4 tsp kosher salt

Directions

- Before you do anything preheat the grill.
- Get a small mixing bowl: Mix in it the garlic, hot pepper, oil and salt. Coat the whole steak with the mix.
- Grease the grill and cook in it the steak for 5 to 7 min on each side.
- Get a small mixing bowl: Toss in it the hearts of palm, tomatoes, onion, hot pepper, cilantro, vinegar and salt to make the salsa.
- Cover the steak with a piece of foil and let it sit for 6 min. Serve it with the tomato salsa.
- Enjoy.

Servings Per Recipe: 4

Timing Information:

Preparation	30 mins
Total Time	50 mins

Nutritional Information:

Calories	464.2
Fat	21.9g
Cholesterol	154.2mg
Sodium	772.7mg
Carbohydrates	13.6g
Protein	52.4g

* Percent Daily Values are based on a 2,000 calorie diet.

Lime Glazed Sirloin

Ingredients

- 4 sirloin steaks, 1 1/2-inches thick
- 1/2 C. lime juice, freshly squeezed
- 1/3 C. dry red wine
- 1 small onion, finely chopped
- 4 garlic cloves, finely chopped
- 2 tsp dried oregano
- 1 bay leaf
- 1 tsp coarse salt
- 1 tsp black pepper

Sauce

- 5 malgueta bell peppers
- 1 tsp salt
- 1 small white onion, finely diced
- 4 large garlic cloves, chopped
- 3 limes, juice of
- 1/2 bunch Italian parsley, chopped

Directions

- Get a food processor: Combine in it the sauce ingredients and process them until they become smooth to make the sauce. Place it aside.
- Lay the steaks on a roasting pan and place it aside.
- Get a small mixing bowl: Mix in it the lime juice with red wine, onion, garlic, oregano, bay leaf, salt and pepper to make the marinade.

- Coat the steaks completely with the marinade and place them in the fridge for at least 4 h.
- Before you do anything preheat the grill and grease it.
- Drain the steaks and cook them for 7 to 9 min on each side. Serve your steaks warm with lime sauce.
- Enjoy.

Servings Per Recipe: 4

Timing Information:

Preparation	15 mins
Total Time	30 mins

Nutritional Information:

Calories	1311.3
Fat	77.6g
Cholesterol	456.0mg
Sodium	1488.8mg
Carbohydrates	18.9g
Protein	125.9g

* Percent Daily Values are based on a 2,000 calorie diet.

Goya Recaito and Seafood Stew

Ingredients

- 2 tbsp olive oil
- 1 onion, chopped fine
- 4 C. chicken stock
- 4 tbsp goya recaito
- 2 tbsp tomato paste
- 14 oz coconut milk
- 12 littleneck clams
- 12 mussels
- 1/2 lb large shrimp
- 2 lobster tails, snipped in half lengthwise before serving
- red pepper, stripped
- green pepper, stripped

Garnishes

- fresh cilantro
- lemon wedge
- lime wedge
- chili oil

Directions

- Place a large saucepan over medium heat. Heat some oil in it. Cook in it the onion for 6 min.
- Stir in the stock, cilantro cooking base, tomato paste and coconut milk. Bring them to a boil. Lower the heat and put on the lid. Let them cook for 22 min.
- Stir in the seafood put on the lid. Let them cook for 6 min. Serve your seafood warm.
- Enjoy.

Servings Per Recipe: 4

Timing Information:

Preparation	20 mins
Total Time	50 mins

Nutritional Information:

Calories	496.8
Fat	30.5g
Cholesterol	121.8mg
Sodium	705.1mg
Carbohydrates	24.8g
Protein	32.2g

* Percent Daily Values are based on a 2,000 calorie diet.

CARAMELIZED BANANAS

Ingredients

- 4 bananas
- 12 tbsp sugar
- 2 C. water

Directions

- Place a heavy saucepan over medium heat. Stir in it the sugar until it completely melts.
- Stir in the water until the sugar dissolves. Stir in the bananas and cook them until they start boiling. Lower the heat and let them cook for 2 h.
- Serve your caramelized bananas with some ice cream.
- Enjoy.

Servings Per Recipe: 4

Timing Information:

Preparation	15 mins
Total Time	2 hrs 15 mins

Nutritional Information:

Calories	251.3
Fat	0.3g
Cholesterol	0.0mg
Sodium	3.5mg
Carbohydrates	64.7g
Protein	1.2g

* Percent Daily Values are based on a 2,000 calorie diet.

SPANISH RICE FRITTERS

Ingredients

- 1 egg, lightly beaten
- 1 small onion, finely chopped
- 1 green scallion, finely chopped
- 1 tbsp fresh parsley, chopped
- 3 -4 tbsp flour
- 1/2 tsp salt
- 1 tbsp milk
- 1 C. leftover cooked rice
- vegetable oil

Directions

- Get a mixing bowl: Whisk in it the egg, onion, scallion, parsley, flour, milk and salt. Add the rice and mix them well.
- Place a large pan over medium heat. Heat about 1/4 inch of oil in the pan.
- Use a tsp to drop the mix in round shape and cook them until they become golden brown.
- Serve your fritters with your favorite dipping sauce.
- Enjoy.

Servings Per Recipe: 1

Timing Information:

| Preparation | 15 mins |
| Total Time | 25 mins |

Nutritional Information:

Calories	37.1
Fat	0.5g
Cholesterol	17.8mg
Sodium	103.9mg
Carbohydrates	6.7g
Protein	1.2g

* Percent Daily Values are based on a 2,000 calorie diet.

Mushroom Strogonoff South American

Ingredients

- 1 tbsp butter
- 2 tbsp butter
- 2 lbs filet mignon
- 1 onion, medium-sized and chopped
- 1/2 lb mushroom, slivered
- 5 tbsp soy sauce
- 1 fluid oz cognac
- 12 oz table cream
- 5 tbsp ketchup
- 2 tbsp mustard
- 1 tbsp flour
- 12 oz milk

Directions

- Sprinkle some salt and pepper over the mignon fillet.
- Place a large skillet over medium heat. Melt 1 tbsp of butter in it. Brown in it the mignon fillet for 2 to 3 min on each side. Place it aside.
- Melt the remaining butter in the same skillet. Sauté in it the onion for 4 min. Stir in the mushroom with the filet mignon and cook them for 6 min.
- Get a large mixing bowl: Whisk in it the table cream, ketchup, mustard, salt and pepper. Add the milk with flour and whisk them until no lumps are found.
- Pour the mix all over the mushroom and filets then let them cook for 7 to 9 min. Once the time is up, serve your creamy stroganoff skillet warm. Enjoy.

Servings Per Recipe: 5

Timing Information:

Preparation	30 mins
Total Time	50 mins

Nutritional Information:

Calories	792.5
Fat	62.9g
Cholesterol	200.7mg
Sodium	1456.8mg
Carbohydrates	15.7g
Protein	41.5g

* Percent Daily Values are based on a 2,000 calorie diet.

BANANAS DO AMOR

Ingredients

- 6 medium bananas, halved lengthwise
- 1/2 C. fresh orange juice
- 1 tbsp fresh lemon juice
- 1/2 C. white sugar
- 1/8 tsp salt
- 2 tbsp butter
- 1 C. flaked coconut

Directions

- Before you do anything preheat the oven to 400 F. Grease casserole dish with some butter.
- Lay the banana slices in the greased dish and place it aside.
- Get a mixing bowl: Whisk in it the orange juice, lemon juice, sugar and salt. Drizzle the mix all over the banana slices.
- Place the dish in the oven and cook it for 16 min. Garnish your banana pan with coconut flakes then serve it with some ice cream.
- Enjoy.

Servings Per Recipe: 12

Timing Information:

| Preparation | 15 mins |
| Total Time | 30 mins |

Nutritional Information:

Calories	135.9
Fat	4.1g
Cholesterol	5.0mg
Sodium	54.3mg
Carbohydrates	25.9g
Protein	0.9g

* Percent Daily Values are based on a 2,000 calorie diet.

Latin Tip Roast

Ingredients

- 1 1/2-2 lbs sirloin tip roast
- 1/2 tsp garlic powder
- 2 onions, sliced
- 1/2 C. beef broth
- 1/2 C. strong black coffee
- 1 tsp salt
- 1/4 tsp oregano
- 1/4 tsp rosemary
- 1/4 tsp pepper
- 2 tbsp flour
- 1 tsp margarine

Directions

- Before you do anything preheat the oven to 350 F.
- Slice the sirloin into small pieces. Toss them in a casserole dish with the garlic powder, onions, liquids and seasonings.
- Cook it in the oven for 60 min. Once the time is up, serve your sirloin gravy with some noodles.
- Enjoy.

Servings Per Recipe: 6

Timing Information:

Preparation	10 mins
Total Time	1 hr 10 mins

Nutritional Information:

Calories	32.5
Fat	0.7g
Cholesterol	0.0mg
Sodium	471.4mg
Carbohydrates	5.6g
Protein	0.9g

* Percent Daily Values are based on a 2,000 calorie diet.

CAMARÃO DE COCO

Ingredients

- 1 lb large shrimp, peeled & deveined
- 1/2 C. chopped onion
- 2 tbsp palm oil
- 1/4 C. chopped garlic
- 1/2 C. chopped fresh cilantro
- 1/2 C. walnuts
- 1/2 C. chopped tomato
- 1 C. chopped broccoli
- 1/4 coconut milk
- 2 tsp paprika
- 1 tsp coriander
- 1/4 C. chopped fresh parsley
- 1 tsp thyme
- 1/2 tsp lemon juice
- 3 dried red chilies, chopped finely
- 1/2 C. rice

Directions

- Place a large saucepan over medium heat. Heat the oil in it. Sauté in it the paprika and the onion for 3 min.
- Stir in the garlic, coriander, thyme, parsley, cilantro, chilies, and walnuts. Let them cook for 4 min.
- Stir in the tomato and let them cook for an extra 6 min.
- Once the time is up, stir in the coconut milk, with broccoli and shrimp. Cook them for 6 min. Serve your shrimp pan warm.
- Enjoy.

Servings Per Recipe: 2

Timing Information:

Preparation	10 mins
Total Time	35 mins

Nutritional Information:

Calories	751.0
Fat	36.3g
Cholesterol	286.4mg
Sodium	1323.5mg
Carbohydrates	66.8g
Protein	43.7g

* Percent Daily Values are based on a 2,000 calorie diet.

Carrot Cake with Cocoa Glaze

Ingredients

- 4-5 medium sized carrots, peeled and chopped
- 1 C. sugar
- 4 eggs
- 1/2 C. vegetable oil
- 2 1/2 C. flour
- 1 pinch salt
- 1 tbsp baking powder

Glaze

- 3 tbsp cocoa
- 2 tbsp butter
- 1/4 C. milk
- 1/2 C. sugar

Directions

- Before you do anything, preheat the oven to 375 F. Grease a baking dish with some butter.
- Get a food processor: Place in it the eggs, sugar, oil, and carrots. Process them until they become smooth.
- Get a large mixing bowl: Combine in it the eggs mix with flour and whisk them until no lumps are found. Add the baking powder and mix them again.
- Pour the batter in the baking pan and cook it in the oven for 32 min.
- Place a heavy saucepan over medium heat. Stir in it the cocoa with butter, milk and sugar. Cook the mix until it starts boiling while stirring all the time.

- Pour the mix all over the cake after it cools down completely. Place the cake in the fridge for at least 30 min then serve it.
- Enjoy.

Servings Per Recipe: 16

Timing Information:

| Preparation | 20 mins |
| Total Time | 50 mins |

Nutritional Information:

Calories	247.3
Fat	9.9g
Cholesterol	50.8mg
Sodium	121.1mg
Carbohydrates	36.1g
Protein	4.0g

* Percent Daily Values are based on a 2,000 calorie diet.

How to Grill a Steak Brazilian Street Style

Ingredients

- 1 untreated cedar plank
- 1/2 C. balsamic vinaigrette dressing
- 1/2 C. finely chopped onion
- 1/2 C. chopped fresh parsley
- 1/4 C. chopped cilantro
- 2 garlic cloves, minced
- 1 dash crushed red pepper flakes
- 1 beef flank steak
- 1 tbsp oil

Directions

- Place the cedar plank in a large dish and top it with a heavy object. Cover the plank with water completely and let it sit for an overnight.
- Get a mixing bowl: Whisk in it the dressing, onions, parsley, cilantro, garlic and red pepper.
- Get a large zip lock bag: Pour in it 1/2 C. of the dressing with the steak. Close the bag and shake the coat the steak with it. Place it in the fridge for 2 h.
- Before you do anything, preheat the grill.
- Drain the steak and cook it for 4 min on each side.

- Drain the cedar plank from the water and grease it with some oil. Place it on the grill and put the steak on it. Put on the lid and cook them for 18 over medium heat.
- Once the time is up, wrap the steak completely with a piece of foil and place it aside to rest for 6 min.
- Serve your grilled steak with the remaining dressing.
- Enjoy.

Servings Per Recipe: 6

Timing Information:

Preparation	4 hrs
Total Time	4 hrs 25 mins

Nutritional Information:

Calories	252.6
Fat	18.7g
Cholesterol	52.2mg
Sodium	38.2mg
Carbohydrates	2.4g
Protein	18.1g

* Percent Daily Values are based on a 2,000 calorie diet.

Caribbean Tilapia Stew

Ingredients

- 1 lime, juice of
- 1 tbsp ground cumin
- 1 tbsp paprika
- 4 garlic cloves
- 1/2 tsp salt
- 1 tsp ground black pepper
- 1 serrano chili, diced
- 1 1/2 lbs tilapia fillets, cut into three by three inch pieces
- 2 tbsp olive oil
- 2 onions, chopped
- 4 large bell peppers, diced
- 1 (16 oz) cans diced tomatoes, drained
- 1 (6 oz) cans tomato paste
- 1 (16 oz) cans whole coconut milk
- 2 tbsp palm oil
- 2 tbsp fish sauce
- 1 bunch fresh cilantro, chopped (optional)
- 6 hard-boiled eggs

Directions

- Get a large mixing bowl: Whisk in it the lime juice, cumin, paprika, garlic, salt and pepper. Add the tilapia pieces and mix them to coat.
- Cover the bowl with a plastic wrap and place it in the fridge for 14 min.
- Place a pot over medium heat. Heat the oil in it. Sauté in it the onion with chilies and cook them for 3 min. Lower the heat and add the tomato paste.

- Stir it the diced tomato with bell peppers and coconut milk. Put on the lid and let it cook for 28 min.
- Once the time is up, stir the tilapia mix into the pot with the 2/3 of the chopped and stemmed cilantro. Let them cook for 7 min.
- Serve your stew warm and garnish it with the hard boiled eggs.
- Enjoy.

Servings Per Recipe: 4

Timing Information:

| Preparation | 15 mins |
| Total Time | 45 mins |

Nutritional Information:

Calories	955.2
Fat	45.0g
Cholesterol	364.8mg
Sodium	1577.6mg
Carbohydrates	93.4g
Protein	51.1g

* Percent Daily Values are based on a 2,000 calorie diet.

Rice Apple Shrimp Salad

Ingredients

- 2 C. cooked rice
- 1 granny smith apple, cut into strips
- 1/2 avocado, sliced
- 1 tbsp chopped pimiento
- 1 C. cooked peas
- 1 tbsp lemon juice
- 1 tbsp white vinegar
- 2 tbsp olive oil
- 1 tsp mustard
- 1 tsp salt
- 1/4 tsp black pepper
- 1/2 head lettuce, shredded
- 3 eggs, hard-boiled
- 1/2 lb shrimp, cooked

Directions

- Get a large mixing bowl. Mix in it the rice with apple, avocado, pimiento and peas.
- Get a small mixing bowl: Whisk in it the lemon juice, vinegar, olive oil, mustard, salt and pepper. Add it to the rice mix and toss them to coat.
- Place the salad in the fridge for 2 h. Serve it with some lettuce, shrimp and hard boiled eggs.
- Enjoy.

Servings Per Recipe: 4

Timing Information:

| Preparation | 30 mins |
| Total Time | 30 mins |

Nutritional Information:

Calories	381.8
Fat	15.0g
Cholesterol	210.9mg
Sodium	1016.0mg
Carbohydrates	43.8g
Protein	18.1g

* Percent Daily Values are based on a 2,000 calorie diet.

Brazilian Long Grain II

Ingredients

- 1 tbsp butter
- 1 C. white rice
- salt

Directions

- Place a large saucepan over medium heat. Heat 1 tbsp of butter in it.
- Stir in the rice and cook it for 3 min. Stir in 2 C. of water with a pinch of salt. Bring it to a boil.
- Put on the cover and let it cook for 16 min over medium heat. Turn off the heat and let it sit for 6 min. Serve it warm.
- Enjoy.

Servings Per Recipe: 3

Timing Information:

| Preparation | 0 mins |
| Total Time | 20 mins |

Nutritional Information:

Calories	262.1
Fat	4.1g
Cholesterol	10.1mg
Sodium	38.1mg
Carbohydrates	50.3g
Protein	4.2g

* Percent Daily Values are based on a 2,000 calorie diet.

Garlicky Chicken with Mango Salsa

Ingredients

- 8 -10 garlic cloves, finely chopped
- salt
- fresh ground black pepper
- 1 lemon, juice and zest of, divided
- 1/2 C. fresh parsley, chopped
- 2 -3 dashes hot sauce
- 4 boneless skinless chicken breasts
- 1 large ripe mango, pitted and chopped
- 4 plum tomatoes, seeded and chopped
- 1/2 medium red onion, chopped
- 1/4 C. cilantro, chopped
- 1 lime, juice of
- 1 C. all-purpose flour
- 2 eggs
- 1/2 C. dried breadcrumbs
- 1/2 C. grated Parmigiano-Reggiano cheese
- 2 -3 dashes nutmeg
- 2 tbsp extra virgin olive oil

Directions

- Before you do anything, preheat the oven to 250 F.
- Get a food processor: Combine in it the garlic with lemon juice, parsley, hot sauce, a pinch of salt and pepper.

Process them several times until they become finely chopped.
- Place the chicken breasts on a working surface and use a kitchen hammer to flatten them until they become 1/4 inch thick.
- Coat the chicken breasts with the garlic mix and place them in the fridge for 12 min.
- Get a small mixing bowl: Toss in it the mango, plum tomatoes, red onion, cilantro, lime juice, some salt and freshly ground black pepper.
- Get a shallow bowl: Whisk in it the eggs with 1 tsp of water.
- Get another mixing bowl: Mix in it the breadcrumbs, grated Parmigiano-Reggiano, nutmeg and lemon zest.
- Place a large pan over medium heat. Heat 2 tbsp of oil in it.
- Dust the chicken breasts with some flour and dip them in the beaten eggs then coat them with the cheese and breadcrumbs mix.
- Cook the chicken breasts in the hot oil for 5 to 6 min on each side. Serve your chicken breasts warm.
- Enjoy.

Servings Per Recipe: 4

Timing Information:

| Preparation | 20 mins |
| Total Time | 40 mins |

Nutritional Information:

Calories	509.5
Fat	14.8g
Cholesterol	181.3mg
Sodium	392.4mg
Carbohydrates	52.8g
Protein	40.9g

* Percent Daily Values are based on a 2,000 calorie diet.

Brazilian Shrimp Skillet

Ingredients

- 20 -30 tiger shrimp
- 2 onions, diced
- 1 green pepper, diced
- 2 tomatoes, diced
- 1 C. chopped fresh cilantro
- 20 oz unsweetened coconut milk
- 5 tbsp palm oil
- salt and pepper
- steamed white rice

Directions

- Place a large skillet over medium heat. Heat the palm oil in it. Sauté in it the prawns for 4 min.
- Stir in the coconut milk, salt, pepper and half the cilantro. Let them cook for 4 min.
- Once the time is up, serve your shrimp skillet warm with some white rice or noodles.
- Enjoy.

Servings Per Recipe: 4

Timing Information:

Preparation	20 mins
Total Time	30 mins

Nutritional Information:

Calories	512.5
Fat	49.0g
Cholesterol	45.6mg
Sodium	70.9mg
Carbohydrates	13.9g
Protein	10.4g

* Percent Daily Values are based on a 2,000 calorie diet.

Latin Flavored Butter

Ingredients

- 1/2 C. unsalted butter, softened
- 2 tsp sugar
- 2 oz orange juice
- 1 orange, zest of
- 1 lemon, zest of
- 2 tbsp Grand Marnier, orange liquor, optional

Directions

- Bring a large saucepan of water to a boil. Cook in it the orange and lemon zest for 2 min. Drain them and finely chop them.
- Get a large mixing bowl: Combine in it all the ingredients. Beat them until they become smooth and creamy. Place the butter in the fridge until ready to serve.
- Enjoy.

Servings Per Recipe: 10

Timing Information:

Preparation	10 mins
Total Time	15 mins

Nutritional Information:

Calories	87.3
Fat	9.2g
Cholesterol	24.4mg
Sodium	1.3mg
Carbohydrates	1.4g
Protein	0.1g

* Percent Daily Values are based on a 2,000 calorie diet.

Catalina's Comfort Cake

Ingredients

- 4 large egg yolks
- 1 C. sugar, divided
- 12 oz cream cheese, at room temp
- 1 1/2 C. heavy cream, well-chilled
- 1 C. rum, optional
- 10 1/2 oz ladyfingers
- 2 C. ripe mangoes, diced
- 2 C. fresh ripe pineapple, diced
- 2 C. ripe papayas, diced
- extra mango
- extra pineapple
- extra papaya

Directions

- Get a large mixing bowl: Mix in it the egg yolks and 2/3 C. sugar until they become pale and creamy.
- Place the bowl on a double boiler and keep mixing it for 5 min until the mix becomes thick. Place the batter aside and let it cool down completely.
- Get a blender: Pour in it the egg batter with the cream cheese. Blend them smooth until they become light and creamy.
- Get a large mixing bowl: Beat in it the heavy cream until it soft peaks. Fold it into the eggs batter. Place it in the fridge until ready to use.
- Place a small saucepan over medium heat. Stir in it the liquor with the remaining 1/3 C. sugar. Let them cook for

6 min. Place it aside to cool down completely to make the syrup.
- Place the ladyfingers in the syrup then drain them and place 1/3 of them in a serving glass dish. Top it with the mango and 1/3 of the cream mix.
- Lay on them 1/3 of the ladyfingers followed by pineapple and 1/3 of the cream mix. Repeat the process using papaya this time.
- Place the cream bowl in the fridge for at least 3 h. Serve it with your favorite toppings.
- Enjoy.

Servings Per Recipe: 8

Timing Information:

| Preparation | 30 mins |
| Total Time | 12 hrs 30 mins |

Nutritional Information:

Calories	685.8
Fat	37.0g
Cholesterol	282.6mg
Sodium	216.8mg
Carbohydrates	66.0g
Protein	9.4g

* Percent Daily Values are based on a 2,000 calorie diet.

Summer Night Banana Coffee Smoothie

Ingredients

- 1 C. skim milk
- 1 tsp cinnamon
- 2 medium bananas
- 2 C. coffee ice cubes
- Splenda sugar substitute, to taste (optional)

Directions

- Get a food processor: combine in it all the ingredients and blend them smooth.
- Serve your coffee shake.
- Enjoy.

Servings Per Recipe: 2

Timing Information:

| Preparation | 5 mins |
| Total Time | 5 mins |

Nutritional Information:

Calories	158.6
Fat	0.7g
Cholesterol	2.4mg
Sodium	73.8mg
Carbohydrates	34.8g
Protein	6.2g

* Percent Daily Values are based on a 2,000 calorie diet.

Savory Pineapple Steaks

Ingredients

- 1 C. brown sugar
- 2 tsp ground cinnamon
- 1 pineapple, peeled, cored, and cut into 6 wedges

Directions

- Before you do anything preheat the grill and grease it.
- Get a small mixing bowl: Mix in it the brown sugar and cinnamon.
- Get a large zip lock bag: Place in it the pineapple slices with the sugar mix. Seal the bag and shake it to coat them.
- Place the pineapple slices on the grill and cook them for 4 to 6 min on each side. Serve them with some ice cream.
- Enjoy.

Servings Per Recipe: 6

Timing Information:

| Preparation | 10 mins |
| Total Time | 20 mins |

Nutritional Information:

Calories	216.9
Fat	0.1g
Cholesterol	0.0mg
Sodium	11.8mg
Carbohydrates	56.4g
Protein	0.8g

* Percent Daily Values are based on a 2,000 calorie diet.

Brazilian Wild Rice

Ingredients

- 6 oz wild rice
- 3/4 C. dry vermouth
- 1/4 C. butter
- 3 tbsp onions, finely chopped
- 1/2 liter mushroom
- 2 eggs, well beaten (optional)
- salt and pepper

Directions

- Before you do anything, preheat the oven to 350 F.
- Prepare the rice according to the directions on the package. Fluff the rice and add to it the dry vermouth. Mix them well.
- Place a heavy saucepan over medium heat. Heat the butter in it until it melts. Sauté in it the onion for 3 min.
- Stir in the mushroom and cook them for 6 min. Add the rice with eggs, a pinch of salt and pepper. Mix them well.
- Pour the mix in a greased casserole dish. Cook it it in the oven for 32 min. Serve your casserole warm.
- Enjoy.

Servings Per Recipe: 4

Timing Information:

| Preparation | 10 mins |
| Total Time | 1 hr 10 mins |

Nutritional Information:

Calories	312.2
Fat	12.1g
Cholesterol	30.5mg
Sodium	108.8mg
Carbohydrates	37.2g
Protein	8.0g

* Percent Daily Values are based on a 2,000 calorie diet.

Latin Leeks with Sweet Vinaigrette

Ingredients

- 4 leeks
- 4 -6 tbsp olive oil
- 1/2 tbsp unsalted butter
- kosher salt & freshly ground black pepper, to taste

Vinaigrette:

- 1/2 C. balsamic vinegar, good quality
- 5 tsp sugar

Directions

- Place a heavy saucepan over medium heat: Whisk in it the balsamic vinegar and sugar. Heat it until it dissolves.
- Cook the mix until it starts simmering. Keep cooking it for 8 min until it reduces by 4 tbsp at least.
- Slice the leeks in half lengthwise and rinse them well. Slice them into strips.
- Place a large pan over medium heat. Heat the butter with oil in it. Sauté in it the leeks for 16 to 20 min.
- Serve your butter leek with the sweet vinegar.
- Enjoy.

Servings Per Recipe: 4

Timing Information:

Preparation	20 mins
Total Time	50 mins

Nutritional Information:

Calories	234.7
Fat	15.2g
Cholesterol	3.8mg
Sodium	25.6mg
Carbohydrates	23.2g
Protein	1.5g

* Percent Daily Values are based on a 2,000 calorie diet.

Vegetable Fiesta

Ingredients

- 2 tbsp olive oil
- 1/4 tsp red pepper flakes
- 1 tsp ground cumin
- 1 tsp ground thyme
- 2 medium sweet potatoes, peeled and chopped
- 1 large leek, cut into 1/2-inch slices (white part only)
- 1 red bell pepper, cut lengthwise into 1/2-inch slices
- 1 yellow bell pepper, cut lengthwise into 1/2-inch slices
- 1 medium yellow onion, sliced into 1/2-inch crescents
- 1 tbsp dark rum
- 2 tbsp fresh lime juice
- 1 large tomatoes, cut lengthwise into 1/2-inch slices
- nonstick cooking spray
- 2 (16 oz) cans black beans, drained and rinsed
- fresh cilantro, chopped
- cooked rice (optional)

Directions

- Place a pot over medium heat. Heat the oil in it.
- Sauté in it the pepper flakes, cumin, and thyme for 30 sec. Stir in the sweet potato and let them cook for 6 min.
- Stir in the leek and let them cook for another 6 min. Add the bell peppers with onion and let them cook for 6 min.

- Stir in the lime juice with rum and let them cook for 7 min. Add the tomato with beans and cook them for 4 min.
- Serve your fiesta stew warm with some rice.
- Enjoy.

Servings Per Recipe: 6

Timing Information:

Preparation	15 mins
Total Time	40 mins

Nutritional Information:

Calories	266.3
Fat	5.4g
Cholesterol	0.0mg
Sodium	32.5mg
Carbohydrates	43.5g
Protein	11.6g

* Percent Daily Values are based on a 2,000 calorie diet.

Caribbean Jumbo Stew

Ingredients

- 1/3 C. olive oil
- 2 medium onions, finely chopped
- 1 small bell pepper, finely chopped
- 2 small tomatoes, finely chopped
- 1 tsp cilantro, finely chopped
- 1 garlic clove, finely chopped
- 1 tbsp tomato paste
- 1 lb jumbo bay shrimp
- 2 tbsp lemon juice
- 1/2 C. coconut milk

Directions

- Place a large pan over medium heat. Heat the oil in it.
- Sauté in it the onion, pepper, tomatoes, cilantro, garlic and tomato paste for 12 min.
- Cook them until they start boiling. Stir in the lemon juice with shrimp and cook them for 3 min.
- Stir in the coconut milk and cook them until they start boiling. Serve your jumbo stew hot with some noodles or rice.
- Enjoy.

Servings Per Recipe: 4

Timing Information:

Preparation	15 mins
Total Time	20 mins

Nutritional Information:

Calories	391.8
Fat	26.6g
Cholesterol	172.8mg
Sodium	223.5mg
Carbohydrates	13.9g
Protein	25.4g

* Percent Daily Values are based on a 2,000 calorie diet.

Simple Portuguese Torte

Ingredients

- 4 tbsp butter
- 1 C. sugar
- 2 C. flour
- 1 tbsp baking powder
- 1 (3 1/2 oz) packages butterscotch pudding mix
- 3 medium eggs
- 1 C. milk
- 1/2 C. flavored syrup
- whipped cream

Directions

- Before you do anything, preheat the oven to 350 F.
- Get a large mixing bowl: Beat in it the sugar with butter until they become light and fluffy.
- Combine in the flour, baking powder and pudding mix. Beat them for 2 minutes straight.
- Combine in the egg yolks with milk. Beat them until they become creamy.
- Get a large mixing bowl: Beat in it the egg whites until their soft peaks. Fold it into the egg yolk mix.
- Pour the batter in a greased baking pan. Cook it in the oven for 52 min.
- Allow the tart to cool down completely then serve it with your favorite toppings.
- Enjoy.

Servings Per Recipe: 8

Timing Information:

| Preparation | 10 mins |
| Total Time | 1 hr |

Nutritional Information:

Calories	351.3
Fat	8.7g
Cholesterol	80.9mg
Sodium	242.1mg
Carbohydrates	62.8g
Protein	6.3g

* Percent Daily Values are based on a 2,000 calorie diet.

South American Street Cocktail

Ingredients

- 2 oz cachaca
- 2 passion fruit
- 1 oz sugar syrup
- 1 oz lemon juice

Directions

- Get a cocktail shaker. Combine in it all the ingredients and shake them well.
- Strain the mix by using a mesh sieve. Pour it in a serving glass with some crushed ice. Serve it with some lime wedges.
- Enjoy.

Servings Per Recipe: 1

Timing Information:

| Preparation | 3 mins |
| Total Time | 3 mins |

Nutritional Information:

Calories	170.4
Fat	0.2g
Cholesterol	0.0mg
Sodium	10.9mg
Carbohydrates	10.8g
Protein	0.9g

* Percent Daily Values are based on a 2,000 calorie diet.

Brazilian Pot Pies

Ingredients

- 2 chicken breasts
- 1 C. tomato sauce
- 1 onion
- 2 garlic cloves
- 1 tsp oregano
- 1 C. canned corn
- 1 tbsp cilantro
- salt and pepper
- 12 tbsp flour
- 1 tbsp baking powder
- 2 tbsp parmesan cheese
- 1/2 tsp salt
- 3 eggs
- 1 1/2-2 C. milk
- 3/4-1 C. oil
- pepper

Dough

Directions

- Place a large pan over medium heat. Heat a splash of oil in it. Cook in it the chicken breasts for 6 to 10 min on each side or until they are done.
- Drain the chicken breasts and stir them back into the pan. Add the tomato sauce, onion, garlic, salt, oregano, pepper, canned corn, and of coarse chopped cilantro.
- Let them cook for 8 min over low heat. Place it aside.
- Before you do anything, preheat the oven to 350 F.
- Get a food processor: Combine in it all the dough ingredients. Process them until they become smooth.

- Spread half of the dough in the bottom of a greased baking dish. Pour the chicken filling all over it. Spread the remaining dough mix all over it.
- Place the pie dish in the oven and cook it for 55 min. Serve it warm with your favorite sauce.
- Enjoy.

Servings Per Recipe: 4

Timing Information:

| Preparation | 40 mins |
| Total Time | 1 hr 25 mins |

Nutritional Information:

Calories	765.2
Fat	55.9g
Cholesterol	200.9mg
Sodium	1075.5mg
Carbohydrates	39.6g
Protein	28.6g

* Percent Daily Values are based on a 2,000 calorie diet.

Homemade Barbeque Sauce

Ingredients

- 1 onion, finely chopped
- 1 green bell pepper, seeded and diced
- 1 tomatoes, seeded and diced
- 1/2 C. olive oil
- 1/2 C. white vinegar

Directions

- Place a large skillet over medium heat. Heat the oil in it with vinegar. Stir in it the remaining ingredients.
- Let them cook for 9 min while stirring them from time to time. Serve your sauce warm.
- Enjoy.

Servings Per Recipe: 1

Timing Information:

| Preparation | 10 mins |
| Total Time | 30 mins |

Nutritional Information:

Calories	1071.9
Fat	108.5g
Cholesterol	0.0mg
Sodium	21.1mg
Carbohydrates	22.5g
Protein	3.1g

* Percent Daily Values are based on a 2,000 calorie diet.

Vanilla Pie

Ingredients

- 1 (170 g) packages vanilla pudding mix
- 2 -3 tbsp instant coffee
- 3 tbsp powdered cocoa mix
- 2 5/8 C. milk
- 1 C. whipping cream
- 1 baked pie shell
- 1/4 C. sliced almonds

Directions

- Place a heavy saucepan over medium heat. Place in it the pudding, coffee, cocoa, and milk. Let them cook until they start boiling while stirring most of the time.
- Turn off the heat and keep stirring mix until it cools down slightly. Pour the mix in a large mixing bowl.
- Cover the bowl with a piece of plastic wrap and place it in the fridge for 60 min.
- Get a large mixing bowl: Beat in it the whipping cream until its soft peaks. Fold the cream into the pudding mixture.
- Pour the mixture into a pie shell and top it with the sliced almonds. Place the pie in the fridge for at least 30 min then serve it.
- Enjoy.

Servings Per Recipe: 8

Timing Information:

| Preparation | 1 hr 40 mins |
| Total Time | 1 hr 40 mins |

Nutritional Information:

Calories	409.8
Fat	23.3g
Cholesterol	52.0mg
Sodium	381.1mg
Carbohydrates	44.5g
Protein	6.1g

* Percent Daily Values are based on a 2,000 calorie diet.

Flan 101

Ingredients

- 1 C. sugar, caramelized
- 1 (14 oz) cans sweetened condensed milk
- 3 eggs
- 2 C. milk
- 1/4 C. parmesan cheese, grated
- 1/4 C. shredded coconut
- 1 tsp vanilla

Directions

- Before you do anything, preheat the oven to 350 F.
- Coat the bottom of the greased ceramic molds with the caramelized sugar. Place them aside until them become hard.
- Get a blender: Combine in it the remaining ingredients and blend them smooth. Pour the mix into the molds.
- Place the molds in a roasting pan and pour some hot water around them that halfway through them.
- Place the pan in the oven and cook them for 1 h 16 min. Allow the flan to cool down for a while then place them in the fridge for an overnight.
- Serve your flan with your favorite toppings.
- Enjoy.

Servings Per Recipe: 12

Timing Information:

| Preparation | 15 mins |
| Total Time | 1 hr 30 mins |

Nutritional Information:

Calories	234.7
Fat	6.8g
Cholesterol	71.6mg
Sodium	116.4mg
Carbohydrates	37.7g
Protein	6.3g

* Percent Daily Values are based on a 2,000 calorie diet.

Chicken Cutlets with Chili Sauce

Ingredients

- cooking oil, for frying
- 1 1/2 kg chicken cutlets
- 1 -2 C. water
- 1 small onion, chopped
- 2 garlic cloves, minced
- salt and pepper
- 1 C. breadcrumbs, or as needed
- 1 C. rice flour
- 2 1/2 C. milk

Garnish:

- 1/2 C. butter
- 3 egg yolks
- 1/4 tsp chili sauce
- salsa

Dough:

Directions

- Place a large skillet over medium heat. Heat the oil in it. Cook in it the chicken cutlets for 3 to 5 min on each side.
- Add 2 C. of water to the skillet and bring them to a boil. Let them cook for 22 min with the lid on.
- Once the time is up, drain the chicken cutlets and cut them into 12 stripes then mince the rest of it. Reserve the cooking liquid.
- Get a large mixing bowl: Mix in it the minced chicken with onion, cloves, salt and pepper.
- Get a large mixing bowl: Combine in it the rice flour with milk and the chicken cooking liquid until you get a soft dough.

- Cut the dough into 12 pieces and flatten them with the palm of your hands.
- Place a flattened piece of dough on a working surface. Place a chicken strip on the end of it with some of the minced chicken mix.
- Roll the dough over the chicken filling in the shape of a cigar. Place it on a lined up baking sheet. Repeat the process with the remaining ingredients.
- Place a large skillet over medium heat. Heat the oil in it. Cook in it the chicken cigars until they become golden brown.
- Serve your chicken cigars with some chili sauce.
- Enjoy.

Servings Per Recipe: 4

Timing Information:

| Preparation | 50 mins |
| Total Time | 1 hr |

Nutritional Information:

Calories	934.8
Fat	37.4g
Cholesterol	400.9mg
Sodium	646.4mg
Carbohydrates	60.9g
Protein	83.7g

* Percent Daily Values are based on a 2,000 calorie diet.

Banana Cloves

Ingredients

- 5 small bananas
- 1 C. sugar
- 2 cinnamon sticks
- 6 whole cloves
- 2 C. water

Directions

- Place a heavy saucepan over low heat. Stir in it all the ingredients.
- Let them cook for 2 h. Serve syrup with some cake or ice cream.
- Enjoy.

Servings Per Recipe: 4

Timing Information:

Preparation	0 mins
Total Time	2 hrs

Nutritional Information:

Calories	305.8
Fat	0.4g
Cholesterol	0.0mg
Sodium	3.6mg
Carbohydrates	78.8g
Protein	1.3g

* Percent Daily Values are based on a 2,000 calorie diet.

Brazilian Casserole

(Shrimp, corn, and Parmesan and Peppers)

Ingredients

- 2 tbsp virgin olive oil
- 1/2 C. chopped yellow onion
- 1/4 C. chopped green bell pepper
- 1 lb fresh jumbo shrimp, cleaned and deveined
- 2 tbsp chopped fresh parsley
- 1/4 C. canned tomato sauce
- 2 tbsp mild salsa
- 1 tsp salt
- 1 tsp fresh ground black pepper
- 2 tbsp all-purpose flour
- 1 C. milk
- 1 tbsp vegetable shortening, for greasing the baking dish
- 2 C. canned cream-style corn
- 1/2 C. grated parmesan cheese

Directions

- Before you do anything, preheat the oven to 375 F.
- Place a large pan over medium heat. Heat the oil in it. Sauté in it the bell pepper with onion for 4 min.

- Stir in the shrimp and parsley. Let them cook for 3 min. Add the tomato sauce, salsa, salt, and pepper. Lower the heat and let them cook for 6 min with the lid on.
- Add the flour followed by the milk gradually while stirring all the time. Turn the heat to medium an let them cook for 4 min.
- Turn off the heat and place the stew aside to cool down for a while.
- Pour the stew in a greased casserole dish. Spread the cream corn over it then top them with the parmesan cheese.
- Place the casserole in the oven and let it cook for 28 min. Once the time is up, serve it hot.
- Enjoy.

Servings Per Recipe: 6

Timing Information:

Preparation	0 mins
Total Time	45 mins

Nutritional Information:

Calories	256.0
Fat	11.7g
Cholesterol	108.3mg
Sodium	1277.5mg
Carbohydrates	22.8g
Protein	17.0g

* Percent Daily Values are based on a 2,000 calorie diet.

Brazilian Potatoes

Ingredients

- 2 lbs small baby potatoes
- 3/4 C. good quality olive oil
- 1/3 C. red wine vinegar
- 1 tsp dried oregano
- 2 -3 garlic cloves, minced
- kosher salt & freshly ground black pepper
- 1/2 C. chopped white onion
- 1 -2 tsp finely minced chili pepper (or to taste)
- 1 C. olive, pitted
- 1/4 C. diced sun-dried tomato
- 1/4 C. chopped parsley

Directions

- Bring a large salted pot of water to a boil. Cook in it the potato until they become soft. Drain them and place them aside.
- Get a large mixing bowl: Mix in it the olive oil, red wine vinegar, oregano, garlic, and salt and pepper. Add the potato and stir them to coat.
- Place the bowl aside until the potato cools down completely. Add to it the onions, chili pepper, olives, sun dried tomatoes, and chopped parsley. Mix them well.
- Place the salad in the fridge for at least 1 h then serve it.
- Enjoy.

Servings Per Recipe: 6

Timing Information:

Preparation	6 hrs
Total Time	6 hrs 25 mins

Nutritional Information:

Calories	385.4
Fat	29.6g
Cholesterol	0.0mg
Sodium	239.7mg
Carbohydrates	28.3g
Protein	3.3g

* Percent Daily Values are based on a 2,000 calorie diet.

Thursday's Latin Lunch Box Salad

Ingredients

- 1 lettuce
- 2 C. pineapple, crunches
- 1/4 C. onion, sliced
- 1 lb tomatoes
- 1/2 C. celery, chopped

Sauce

- 1/2 C. plain nonfat yogurt
- 1/4 C. olive oil
- 1 lime, juice of
- salt and pepper

Garnish

- 1/2 C. peanuts, rough chopped

Directions

- Get a food processor: Combine in it the sauce ingredients and blend them smooth.
- Get a large mixing bowl: Mix in it all the salad ingredients. Add to it the sauce and toss them to coat.
- Serve your salad with some peanuts or your other favorite toppings.
- Enjoy.

Servings Per Recipe: 4

Timing Information:

| Preparation | 15 mins |
| Total Time | 15 mins |

Nutritional Information:

Calories	310.6
Fat	22.9g
Cholesterol	0.6mg
Sodium	44.6mg
Carbohydrates	22.8g
Protein	8.1g

* Percent Daily Values are based on a 2,000 calorie diet.

Kielbasa Stew

Ingredients

- 1 lb beef stew meat, seasoned with salt and pepper
- 1 tbsp vegetable oil
- 8 oz kielbasa, sliced into 1/2 inch thick rounds
- 1/4 C. orange juice
- 1 1/2 C. diced onions
- 1 (14 1/2 oz) cans diced tomatoes
- 1 (15 oz) cans black beans, drained and rinsed
- 1 (15 oz) cans black beans, drained and rinsed and pureed
- 2 tbsp minced garlic
- 1 tbsp chili powder
- 1 tbsp red wine vinegar
- sliced jalapeno
- orange wedge
- orange zest

Directions

- Place a large pan over high heat. Heat the oil in it. Cook in it the stew meat in batches for 6 min until it browned. Drain it and place it aside.
- Cook the kielbasa in the same pan for 4 min per batch. Drain it and placei it aside.
- Stir the orange juice in the same pan to deglaze it.
- Stir the onions, tomatoes, beans, garlic, and chili powder in a slow cooker. Add to it the stew meat with orange juice, beans, a pinch of salt and pepper.

- Put on the lid and cook the stew on high for 5 h.
- Once the time is up, stir in the vinegar. Serve your stew hot.
- Enjoy.

Servings Per Recipe: 6

Timing Information:

Preparation	30 mins
Total Time	4 hrs 30 mins

Nutritional Information:

Calories	409.8
Fat	16.9g
Cholesterol	73.2mg
Sodium	429.9mg
Carbohydrates	34.5g
Protein	31.6g

* Percent Daily Values are based on a 2,000 calorie diet.

Creamy Coconut Cassava and Shrimp

Ingredients

- 1 lb yucca root, Peeled and chopped into 1inch pieces
- 2 tbsp olive oil
- 2 medium onions, chopped fine
- 4 ripe tomatoes, chopped fine
- 2 lbs small cooked peeled prawns
- 60 g coriander, chopped
- 100 g coconut cream, grated
- 1 1/2-3 tbsp palm oil
- 1 lime, quartered

Directions

- Bring a large salted pot of water to a boil. Cook in it the yucca root for 38 min. Drain it and mash it.
- Place a large pan over medium heat. Heat a splash of oil in it. Sauté in it the onion for 4 min.
- Stir in the tomato and cook them for 6 min. Add the prawns with coconut cream, a pinch of salt and pepper. Stir them until the cream melts.
- Stir in the coriander and mashed Yucca. Let them cook for 6 min. Stir in the palm oil. Serve your shrimp pan with some rice or noodles.
- Enjoy.

Servings Per Recipe: 4

Timing Information:

Preparation	15 mins
Total Time	35 mins

Nutritional Information:

Calories	589.2
Fat	18.9g
Cholesterol	285.7mg
Sodium	1324.2mg
Carbohydrates	70.8g
Protein	34.8g

* Percent Daily Values are based on a 2,000 calorie diet.

Chipotle Shrimps

Ingredients

- 3 tsp olive oil
- 1 onion, finely chopped
- 6 tomatoes, peeled, diced
- 1/4 C. fresh flat-leaf parsley, finely chopped
- 1 lb shrimp, shelled, deveined, and cut into bite size pieces
- 1/2 tsp ground black pepper
- 1 tbsp butter
- 1 tbsp flour
- 1 (13 1/2 oz) cans coconut milk
- 1/2 tsp salt
- 1 small dried red pepper, minced
- 1 tsp dried chipotle powder

Directions

- Place a pot over medium heat. Heat a splash of oil in it. Sauté in it the onion for 3 min. Add the parsley with tomato and cook them for 6 min.
- Stir in the shrimp and cook them for 4 min. Add the melted butter with coconut milk, a pinch of salt and pepper then stir them well.
- Stir in the chipotle and cook them for an extra 4 min. Serve your stew warm with some rice.
- Enjoy.

Servings Per Recipe: 4

Timing Information:

Preparation	15 mins
Total Time	30 mins

Nutritional Information:

Calories	379.5
Fat	28.3g
Cholesterol	150.5mg
Sodium	993.9mg
Carbohydrates	15.7g
Protein	19.7g

* Percent Daily Values are based on a 2,000 calorie diet.

Pumpkin Bonbons

Ingredients

- 1 C. pumpkin puree
- 1 C. granulated sugar
- 2 C. grated coconut
- 1/4 tsp cinnamon
- 1/3 tsp ground cloves
- butter, for greasing
- confectioners' sugar, for dusting

Directions

- Place a large heavy saucepan over medium heat. Combine in it all the ingredients and cook them until they become slightly thick or reach 238 to 245 degrees F.
- Pour the mix in a greased baking dish to lose heat.
- Once the time is up, shape the mix into balls and coat them with some confectioner sugar. Serve them or store them in airtight containers.
- Enjoy.

Servings Per Recipe: 1

Timing Information:

Preparation	10 mins
Total Time	40 mins

Nutritional Information:

Calories	38.6
Fat	2.2g
Cholesterol	0.0mg
Sodium	1.3mg
Carbohydrates	4.9g
Protein	0.2g

* Percent Daily Values are based on a 2,000 calorie diet.

Brazilian Strawberry Tart

Ingredients

- 1 (12 oz) cans sweetened condensed milk
- 24 oz milk
- 3 egg yolks
- 2 tbsp cornstarch
- 1 (8 oz) packages strawberry Jell-O gelatin dessert
- 1 C. boiling water
- 1 C. cold water
- 3 egg whites
- 6 tbsp sugar

Directions

- Place a large heavy saucepan over medium heat. Combine in it the condensed milk, milk, egg yolks, and corn starch. Let them cook until they melt and become creamy.
- Turn off the heat and let them mix lose heat for a while.
- Dissolve the Jell-O completely in some cold water then transfer it to a mixing bowl. Add to it 1 C. of hot water and stir it.
- Get a large mixing bowl: Mix in it the eggs with sugar until their soft peaks. Add the Jell-O and beat them until they become smooth.
- Spread the condensed cream mix in the bottom of a serving glass dish. Top it with the Jell-O mix and place it in the fridge for at least 3 to 4 h.
- Serve it with your favorite toppings.
- Enjoy.

Servings Per Recipe: 10

Timing Information:

Preparation	30 mins
Total Time	2 hrs 30 mins

Nutritional Information:

Calories	297.7
Fat	6.8g
Cholesterol	78.4mg
Sodium	204.4mg
Carbohydrates	51.6g
Protein	8.6g

* Percent Daily Values are based on a 2,000 calorie diet.

Spicy Salmon Fillets

Ingredients

- 4 salmon fillets
- 1/2 large lemon, juice of
- 1/2 large orange, juice of
- salt and pepper
- 1 whole orange, zest of
- 2 tbsp brown sugar
- 1 tbsp chili powder
- 1 clove garlic, minced
- 2 tbsp butter, melted

Directions

- Mix the fruit juices with a pinch of salt and pepper in a large baking pan.
- Place in it the salmon fillets and place them aside to sit for 20 min.
- Before you do anything, preheat the oven to 425 F.
- Cover the bottom of a baking dish with a piece of foil and coat it with some butter.
- Get a small mixing bowl: Mix in it the orange zest, brown sugar, chili powder and minced garlic.
- Drain the salmon fillets from the marinade and coat them with the sugar mix. Place them in the foiled cover pan.
- Melt the remaining butter and pour it all over the salmon fillets. Cook them in the oven for 10 to 14 min. Serve them warm.
- Enjoy.

Servings Per Recipe: 4

Timing Information:

| Preparation | 25 mins |
| Total Time | 35 mins |

Nutritional Information:

Calories	493.9
Fat	20.0g
Cholesterol	161.5mg
Sodium	324.2mg
Carbohydrates	9.5g
Protein	65.6g

* Percent Daily Values are based on a 2,000 calorie diet.

Simple Brazilian Long Grain III

Ingredients

- 2 C. long-grain white rice
- 3 tbsp oil
- 1/4 C. finely chopped onion
- 3 large garlic cloves, finely chopped
- 3 C. hot water
- 1 C. hot chicken stock
- 1 tsp salt
- fresh ground black pepper

Directions

- Rub the rice under some water to rinse it.
- Place a pot over medium heat. Heat the oil in it. Sauté in it the onion for 2 min.
- Stir in the garlic and cook them for 30 sec. Stir in the rice with a pinch of salt and cooked for 2 min.
- Add the hot with broth and cook them until they start simmering.
- Lower the heat and put on the lid. Cook the rice for 24 to 26 min. Fluff it with a fork and serve it hot.
- Enjoy.

Servings Per Recipe: 6

Timing Information:

| Preparation | 15 mins |
| Total Time | 40 mins |

Nutritional Information:

Calories	297.0
Fat	7.4g
Cholesterol	0.0mg
Sodium	519.2mg
Carbohydrates	50.6g
Protein	5.4g

* Percent Daily Values are based on a 2,000 calorie diet.

Estofado de Pescado
(Coconut Sea Stew)

Ingredients

- 1/3 C. fresh lime juice
- 1/2 tsp salt
- 1/2 tsp fresh ground black pepper
- 2 garlic cloves, minced
- 1 (1 1/2 lb) sea bass cut into 1/2-inch wide strips
- 1 1/2 lbs large shrimp, peeled and deveined
- 2 tbsp olive oil
- 2 C. finely chopped onions
- 1 C. finely chopped green bell pepper
- 1 C. finely chopped red bell pepper
- 3/4 C. minced green onion (about 1 bunch)
- 5 garlic cloves, minced
- 1 bay leaf
- 2 C. chopped tomatoes (about 2 large)
- 1/2 C. minced fresh cilantro, divided
- 2 (8 oz) bottles clam juice
- 1 (14 1/2 oz) cans reduced-sodium fat-free chicken broth
- 1 C. light coconut milk
- 1/4 tsp ground red pepper

Directions

- Get a large mixing bowl: Stir in it the lime juice with salt pepper, garlic, sea bass, shrimp and olive oil. Place it in the fridge for 35 min.

- Place a large pot over medium heat. Heat the oil in it. Sauté in it the onion, bell peppers, green onions, garlic, and bay leaf for 7 min.
- Stir in the tomato and cook them for 3 min on high heat.
- Stir in 1/4 C. cilantro, clam juice, and broth. Cook them until they start boiling. Lower the heat and cook them for 12 min.
- Drain the bay leaf and discard it.
- Get a food processor: pour it 1/3 of the mixture and process them until they become smooth. Stir it back into the pot with coconut milk.
- Cook them until they start boiling over high heat. Stir in the shrimp and sea bass mix then cook for 4 min.
- Serve your stew hot with some rice and cilantro.
- Enjoy.

Servings Per Recipe: 6

Timing Information:

| Preparation | 30 mins |
| Total Time | 1 hr |

Nutritional Information:

Calories	325.1
Fat	8.4g
Cholesterol	189.7mg
Sodium	1198.5mg
Carbohydrates	22.7g
Protein	38.9g

* Percent Daily Values are based on a 2,000 calorie diet.

Zesty Veggies and Potato Salad

Ingredients

- 1 lb red potatoes
- 1 green onion, chopped
- 1/4 limes or 1/4 lemon
- 3 tbsp mayonnaise
- 1 stalk celery, chopped
- 1/2 carrot, grated
- salt and pepper

Directions

- Bring a salted pot of water to a boil. Cut the potatoes into wedges and cook them until they become tender. Drain them.
- Get a large mixing bowl: Toss in it the hot potato with lemon juice and toss them to coat.
- Add the onion with mayonnaise, celery, carrot, a pinch of salt and pepper. Toss them to coat. Place the salad in the fridge for at least 45 min then serve it.
- Enjoy.

Servings Per Recipe: 6

Timing Information:

| Preparation | 10 mins |
| Total Time | 30 mins |

Nutritional Information:

Calories	87.8
Fat	2.5g
Cholesterol	1.9mg
Sodium	66.1mg
Carbohydrates	14.9g
Protein	1.6g

* Percent Daily Values are based on a 2,000 calorie diet.

THANKS FOR READING! JOIN THE CLUB AND KEEP ON COOKING WITH 6 MORE COOKBOOKS....

http://bit.ly/1TdrStv

To grab the box sets simply follow the link mentioned above, or tap one of book covers.

This will take you to a page where you can simply enter your email address and a PDF version of the box sets will be emailed to you.

Hope you are ready for some serious cooking!

http://bit.ly/1TdrStv

Come On...
Let's Be Friends :)

We adore our readers and love connecting with them socially.

Like BookSumo on Facebook and let's get social!

[Facebook](#)

And also check out the BookSumo Cooking Blog.

[Food Lover Blog](#)

Printed in Great Britain
by Amazon